Meditation Made Me Do It

how sitting to do nothing can change everything

James Brown

Humans Being Press 2025

Humans Being Press

ISBNs: 979-8-9926251-0-3 (paperback) 979-8-9926251-1-0 (ebook)
Cover and book design by Molly Mortimer, Mayfly book design
Library of Congress Number: 2025922955

First Edition

To Yvette . . .

Thanks for your love and support,

for staying with me,

and for believing in me

when I didn't.

It's been quite a ride.

I love you.

Contents

Five things to know about this book

1. For the last several years I've written a weekly *monday meditations* newsletter that was sent out to my students, and to anyone who was curious about what and how I teach. The posts were often inspired by what was happening in the world, or in my life, and were written in a loose, conversational style that frequently included call-backs to previous posts, hyperlinks to YouTube videos and other cultural ephemera, and questions that readers could answer just by replying to the email.

   Now that they've been collected into a book, I've attempted to recreate that conversational feel by adding side notes in biggish circles inset into the text of some essays. I hope you find them helpful. And while you probably don't have my email address, I'd *love* to hear from you, so visit vedicpathmeditation.com and you should find a way to reach me. That's also a good place to reach out if you're curious about learning, or if you want support for your practice.

2. There are some curse words in this book, and a few references to politics. Hope you're not offended.

3. Grammar Police be warned: my use of punctuation . . . including those three little dots, is different from what's prescribed in style books. I frequently leave out commas, enjoy making up words, and am haphazard in my use of em dashes and parentheses. And I start a lot of sentences with "And."

Fragments abound.

4. Over the course of about three years, my wife was diagnosed with a debilitating lung condition, got sicker and sicker, almost died, got a lung transplant, was in and out of the ICU for a few months, recovered, and is, at the time of publication (fingers crossed), doing great. There are six essays in the collection that reference her medical adventure, starting with #59— *Dis-Ease,* which also includes notes about the other essays in that series. I mention this in case you want to avoid them (I would understand), or in case they might be particularly resonant with your personal experience.

5. Meditation is a powerful, life-changing practice, but it's not a cure-all by any means. Whenever I'm working with a student and issues come up that are beyond my scope I strongly encourage them to seek help from a medical professional, and would encourage you to do the same.

Dad,

Comparison is the thief of joy. Make a book you are happy about.

— Logan (the author's son)

Introduction

This is not a book about how to meditate, but about *why*.

And I mean, *really* why.

Which means not for the reasons you'll find documented in all those scientific studies — all the findings of lower blood pressure, better digestion, better sleep, fewer sick days, reduced risk of depression, heart disease and . . . well, it's a long list.

And by all means, yay for all that. Who doesn't want to be healthier? But in my years of teaching, the most gratifying reports I get are the ones from people who've finally found a way to make meditation a habit and are enjoying the real-life benefits that no scientific study could measure.

"I feel my life just flows better."

"I don't beat myself up in my head as much as I used to, and spend way less time trapped in analysis paralysis."

"Things that really used to bother me don't bother me so much anymore."

"Colors seem brighter, food tastes better . . . the world has come more alive."

"I enjoy all the little moments of life I used to be too overwhelmed to notice."

"There are fewer nights when I get home and need a drink to take the edge off."

"I'm more present for the people and situations that really matter to me."

"I still get mad at my husband sometimes, he can still be an a-hole, but since I learned to meditate I just don't stay mad."

The last one makes me smile because it's an actual quote from my wife, Yvette, from a conversation she was having with her best friend about a year after we learned to meditate, long before I got the very odd idea to become a teacher.

She was talking about how meditation had helped us find the calm and clarity we needed to get through a very rough patch in our marriage, and her friend, who'd known all the nitty-gritty details of our troubles (as best friends tend to do) asked, "So . . . you guys never fight anymore or what?"

Yvette laughed because, of course we still fight now and then. Being married and raising kids is still a challenge, and I can still be, as she was quick to point out, a bit of an ass.

From my perspective, I went from being one of those guys who might complain to his buddy, "Dude, my wife's been mad at me for a week . . . for nothing!" to admitting that now she might be mad at me for an hour . . . for something.

And that, my friends, is what I call progress.

Reports from the corner of Meditation and Life.

Meditation has the power to change everything in our lives, because it polishes and expands the lens of consciousness through which we experience everything. It gives us a whole new perspective, which changes how we see things, how we think about things, how we react to things, and ultimately, it changes how we show up in the world in our everyday lives.

Meditation Made Me Do It is a collection of reports from that polished and expanded perspective, from what I like to call the corner of Meditation and Life.

The essays range from tips on how to be more present in the midst of everyday distractions, to the squishy Zen of picking up dog poop, to deep reflections on the illusion of separateness and the ground of being.

Yes, there really is an essay about picking up poop—see #17 in the table of contents—and it's one of my favorites.

Some take their inspiration from ancient wisdom traditions and some from pop culture.

Some are inspired by questions students have asked, some by quotes from Rumi, Alan Watts, Mark Twain, Dr. Seuss and other great sages . . . and some are inspired by weird things my kids have done or said.

I'm not an enlightened master (whatever that is), and don't pretend to have everything figured out. I'm a guy who learned to meditate, found a way to make it stick, and whose moment-to-moment experience of life is so much better, in so many ways, for having done so.

And I believe meditation could do the same for you.

Which is why I write, and why I teach, and why I hope you enjoy this book.

With love, James

When an Egg Cracks From the Inside

There are two ways an egg can crack.

If it cracks from the inside, that's growth. If it cracks from the outside, something's getting eaten.

There are a lot of experiences we can dive headlong into, sprinting toward self-improvement.

Crash diets.

Killer bootcamps.

Immersive, "life-changing" weekend workshops that have you screaming at the top of your lungs, straining to make the sound of the inner, unstoppable you.

But a few weeks later . . . life is pretty much the same. (And *that's* why you simply must sign up for the weekly coaching program!)

That's change forced from the outside in. From the top down.

For the story of why my first foray into meditation flopped, go to #24—An Unfair Comparison.

For me learning to meditate was an experience of the egg cracking from the inside.

I stumbled upon a friend's blog post in which he talked about meditation in a way that seemed different than the sit-super-still-and-focus-your-face-off style I'd tried and failed at in some austere Zen centers 15 years earlier.

I was skeptical, but curious. That quiet inner voice whispered, "check it out."

Crack.

I met a teacher who resonated with me. Seemed like a normal guy . . . no flowing robes, no beads, no hypnotizing Guru eyes. He was even a baseball fan, like me.

Crack.

During the course he offered I learned that I didn't have to fight my mind to meditate, that I didn't have to sit rigidly like a monk. It was about allowing myself to be in meditation, not trying so hard.

I found the practice easy, which meant I could do it.

Crack.

And so I did it. Every day.

Crack, crack, crack.

And the changes, which have been truly life-changing, came at their own pace.

Shifts I never sought, never could've imagined possible.

It's been, and continues to be, a fascinating ride.

Thanks to all my teachers along the way.

Thanks to all who've given me the honor of being a teacher.

2

Your Flavor of Yummy

Way back when I was a creative director in advertising, my job was to persuade people that my client's brand was better, faster, more durable, more stylish, more advanced, more whatever than its competitors.

It was just how the game was played.

When I became a meditation teacher I thought I'd left all that behind. So I was somewhat surprised to discover that a similar kind of "brand" one-upmanship was a big part of the spiritual game, with teachers of different disciplines making bold, largely unsubstantiated claims about why their practice was better, why their bliss was deeper, or purer, or better at obliterating the ego, or that their teaching lineage stretched further back into antiquity.

And to be candid, for a while I was one of those teachers. Because the man I did teacher training with would often bluntly demean other practices, saying things like "What I'm giving you is Supreme Knowledge," and comparing our teacher-training to "a PhD program," while others were "teaching kindergarten."

Because I idolized my teacher (for a while, I'm over it now), I believed him and would say similar things, but usually not so overtly.

As I moved further along the path I saw that what he was saying wasn't true, and so I stopped saying those things.

I saw that different spiritual practices resonate with different people at different times. And just because you find a practice that works now doesn't mean it will be your practice forever. Times, things and people all change, and so will our practice . . . if we don't hold on too tightly.

A while back I had the pleasure of co-teaching a day-long meditation retreat with a Zen priest. She wore robes. I wore jeans and a hoodie.

She emphasized good postural discipline and demonstrated the best way to place your hands so that the fingertips touch very lightly. I said that you can slouch and scratch your way to enlightenment and that it doesn't matter where you place your hands.

She taught us to focus on the breath and to keep the eyes open. I taught closing the eyes and allowing thoughts to flow, without focusing or concentrating, using the breath like a diving board, not an anchor.

But while before I would've focused on those differences, I came away from the day happy to have discovered all the ways in which our teachings overlapped and complemented each other. It was a wonderful experience of mutual respect and affection, and I think the participants who shared the day with us felt that way too.

Now, whenever I hear people jousting about the superiority of their guru, or their spiritual practice, or their preferred plant medicine, or maybe just boasting that their favorite productivity hack is the most

See #48—
What's The Rush
for a deeper dive
on spiritual
hucksterism.

productive, I like to imagine they're talking about their favorite flavor of ice cream. And I think how absurd it would be to boldly stride into the local ice cream parlor and loudly proclaim the clear superiority of Rocky Road over Pralines and Cream . . . no matter how obvious it is to me.

Because you can't have an ice cream parlor with just one flavor of ice cream.

Luckily, spirituality also comes in lots of different flavors. Sometimes you can even combine them, with two or three scoops piled on top of your cone.

Or cup . . . whichever you prefer.

But a nice crisp waffle cone is most definitely the way to go, and will surely lead to a more tantalizing taste of nirvana :)

3

The Unresisting Wrestler

Imagine a match in which one of the wrestlers just sat there, refusing to wrestle.

It'd be over quickly, and it wouldn't be much of a show. The crowd might start throwing things.

B-O-R-I-N-G!

That's pretty similar to how I teach meditation.

This surprises people, who have usually come to learn hoping meditation will be a tool to help them subdue their unwanted, useless, annoying, anxious thinking.

(No one, in my many years of teaching, has ever said, "I'm here to meditate because I have exactly the right number of thoughts in my head." Everyone has too many thoughts. It's not just you.)

So they try listening to guided meditations, using someone else's soothing voice to distract themselves from the harsher voice in their heads.

They try focusing and concentrating. They try telling themselves to think this thought, and not to think that thought.

But battling thoughts with other thoughts is just more thinking.

When you fight your mind you lose, every time.

What if you stopped fighting?

What if you let everything be as it is?

What if instead of wrestling with thoughts you sat down and simply allowed them flow?

It wouldn't be much of a wrestling match . . . which is pretty much the point.

4

The Universe Is Not
Out To Get Anybody

A woman arrived about 15 minutes late for a workshop. She looked frazzled and stressed out, and was walking with quick, timid steps, the way people who feel bad about being late move.

She apologized, both to the people she was walking past and to me, saying, "Sorry . . . it's been one of those weeks . . . you know? The universe is totally out to get me."

I stood and bowed deeply.

"Much respect," I said.

"Huh?" she asked.

"Well," I said, "the universe is fairly large and you, in comparison, are pretty small. So if the universe is out to get you . . . and you haven't been got?"

I bowed again.

And she, thankfully, laughed.

Because clearly, the universe is not out to get anybody.

But it can sure feel like that, right?

I know I've felt that way. Used to feel that way a lot.

Why?

Usually (actually always), it was because my idea of how things should be going was out of alignment with what was actually happening. Things weren't going my way. I was having a bad day/week/year.

Not only didn't the universe not have my back, it was kind of kicking my ass.

I'm guessing you can relate.

But the undeniable truth is that things simply are the way they are. The universe is never out of alignment, no matter what my thinking tells me.

Whenever it feels differently, I have a choice.

1. Put on my cranky pants and complain.

2. Get present, and get in flow with what is happening.

I'll be honest. I still do my fair share of bitching and moaning. But way less than before, and I bounce back more quickly. I credit daily meditation and an evolving understanding of how the world works.

And what I've found is that the less I complain the quicker I can rise to the occasion and have an adaptive response to whatever the situation might be.

I can bring more of my best to more of my life.

And so can you.

5

No Slow Cheetahs

Every cheetah is really, really fast.

(OK, technically you might run across a very old, or sick, or injured cheetah . . . but you get the point.)

And the reason is simple: evolution doesn't over-engineer its creations. It doesn't endow creatures with more capacity than they need. So cheetahs evolved to have a musculoskeletal structure, and lung capacity, and a massive heart, and non-retractable claws, and a skull shaped like one of those aerodynamic helmets Olympic downhill skiers wear, and a whole host of other tweaks in the genome . . . all of which add up to them being very, very fast.

So it makes you (or at least it makes me) wonder . . .

Why is it, with the most complex and best brains on the planet, that we *homo sapiens* spend such a huge amount of time being utterly confused about what to do?

You'd think that a confused human would be as rare as a slow cheetah. But that's clearly not the case.

It's so common we have a phrase for it: we call it *analysis-paralysis*, and it gets us twisted up in the tightest of knots.

And a good chunk of the spiritual self-help industrial marketplace is about selling you ways to untangle those knots, especially in relationships. There are so many books and podcasts and videos and . . .

I'm not saying that it's not helpful advice.

I mean, if you have a knot, whether it's in your shoelace or in your most intimate relationship, there are two approaches. You can either figure out how to loosen things up to get it untied, or you take some scissors, cut through it and start over with a new pair of shoelaces, or a new relationship.

But, as I always like to do, it's good to take a step back and ask some broader questions: Why do we get tied up in so many knots? Why do we get so paralyzed?

There are a lot of factors: Anxiety. Fear of making a mistake, of being criticized or made fun of. And stress, of course, which activates the amygdala and intensifies our anxiety and fear.

It's hard to think clearly when your nervous system is jacked up on stress chemistry.

But I think the most overlooked factor is that from the time we're very small we get it drilled into us that we should be able to "figure things out." We're taught to discount our gut feelings and really think things through to make sure we make the right decision.

So we end up overthinking everything.

There was a time when my vision of Hell on Earth was three viable options. I would grind away, making pro/con lists, I would bug my friends asking for their opinion over and over again, doing everything I could think of to ensure I made the right choice . . . but no matter how long I took and how many friends I annoyed, I often made the wrong one. And then had to suffer through waves of buyer's remorse and self-recrimination.

Sound familiar?

But I don't have that problem so much anymore. Especially not with the really big decisions. Not because I got better at figuring everything out, but because I stopped trying quite so hard.

And it's also because I learned to meditate, which gave me tool is could use to get past the cluttered surface of the mind and tune into that inner navigational beacon which is meant to guide us through life. You might call it a deeper knowingness, or gut instinct, or the word of God . . . whatever you choose to call it, the point is we all have it.

But here's where another important principle of neurophysiology comes into play: the one that says our abilities don't get stronger if we don't use them. This is why your muscles don't get bigger if you stop working out. It's why your ability to speak a second language fades if you don't speak it. And it's why if you stop tuning into that internal guidance system you stop being able to be guided by it.

For an amazing true story about this internal guidance system in action see #13— Go to Sausalito.

You get stuck in analysis paralysis, struggling to figure out your life.

Meditation is what got me out of the trap. But other things work to help consistently get in touch with our inner navigational beacon. It could be prayer. Free-flow journaling. Or just taking long, meandering walks with your phone on silent mode, not listening to a podcast or an audiobook.

Now, don't get me wrong, I love audiobooks, especially when walking our dog on the beach, but I also really appreciate those times when I choose to not fill my head with other people's ideas, no matter how delightful or entertaining they might be.

It's nice to clear the decks and allow yourself to be open to whatever might arise from within.

But whatever might work for you, it's important to first acknowledge what doesn't work.

The intellect is an amazing tool. It's useful for solving math problems or setting the agenda for a conference.

But it's a terrible navigator. Meaning if you're trying to use the power of the rational, analytical mind to figure out who to love, or what to do with your life, or where to find purpose or meaning . . . any of the truly big questions in life, you're using the wrong tool for the job.

6

The Witness for the Prosecution

I meet a lot of very type-A, very successful people who present as "happy." Their social media feeds are full of smiles, sunsets, and great times with friends. But inside, they confide, they are chewing themselves up, a constant stream of negative self-talk, like this angry voice yelling at them inside their own heads.

I call that voice "the witness for the prosecution," because it's forever raising objections, making accusations and trying to rile up the jury. But, by whatever name we call it, we all hear it. It's that undermining, undercutting, belittling voice that chirps away, usually more loudly when we're stressed or anxious . . .

She won't dance with you.
You suck.
That's a stupid idea.
You should be more organized.
You should save more money.
They'll never promote you.
You'll never lose weight/stop drinking/stop gambling/stop whatever.
You don't deserve happiness/love/attention/whatever.

And so on . . .

I can identify because I used to beat myself up a lot. And what made it worse was that I believed the things that the angry voice inside my head was telling me. After all, who knew me better than . . . me?

I tried lots of things to drown that voice out. Exercise worked, for a while. Drinking worked, for a while. Lots of things worked . . . for a while.

But the voice always came back, often with fresh evidence of my recent suckyness to shove in my face.

Then I learned to meditate in the flow approach I now teach, and within the first couple of sessions I was able to connect with something deeper and calmer. I could see that I was something other than that voice. I could see that it wasn't me, just a part of me.

So I stopped trying to drown it out, stopped arguing with it. Many years and several thousand meditations later, I still hear that voice—thankfully less often and less loudly—because it never goes away completely. I just don't identify with it. And as a result, it has way less power.

Sometimes in my meditation classes people say, "I didn't want to be thinking those thoughts." Or, "I was having too many thoughts."

And I ask, "What part of you didn't want to be thinking those thoughts? What part of you judged that there were too many thoughts?"

Huh?

I explain that clearly there's some part of us that is thinking those allegedly undesired or excessive thoughts. And then there's the part of us that doesn't think we should be.

That part, the one that's saying you shouldn't be thinking those thoughts, that's the witness for the prosecution. The inner bully. And often, as that voice gets louder and more insistent, the asshole.

But that voice is not you, just a part of you. More precisely, it's the ego, jacked up on stress hormones, telling you to watch it, that the world is a dangerous place, and you need to get your act together . . . or else.

The ego's job is to keep you alive. To help you make critical decisions like whether to fight or flee . . . IN THE CASE OF AN ACTUAL EMERGENCY.

But when we're under stress, the mind is constantly scanning the environment for threats. And it sees them, everywhere, and most of the time it's wrong. So we end up having a reaction to life that is, shall we say, a bit over-the-top. Like screaming at your phone. Or traffic. Or yourself because you forgot to buy avocados.

OK, so what can you do about it . . . today?

1. Be a detective. Start to notice when that voice is getting cranked up.

2. Take a breath . . . and then hold it for just a few seconds . . . then release. Just doing that can often allow enough of a pause to give you a bit of perspective. It's just a voice in your head. It's not you. And 99% of the time it's not even true. You're not under attack. (Certainly not when you're meditating.)

3. Stop arguing with that voice. Arguing sucks you in. Arguing is stressful. It jacks you up on adrenaline and your inner experience quickly becomes a shouting match of "You shut up!" "No, you shut up!"

4. Find something you can do on a daily basis to reduce the level of stress in your life. For me, the flow approach to meditation was the game-changer. It's the most accessible, enjoyable, and doable thing I've ever found. But it's not the only thing that can reliably,

consistently reduce the caustic effect stress has on your life. Find something you can do . . . and do it. That voice will certainly raise objections to whatever you try, telling you that it won't work for you, or that you won't be able to do it right, or long enough.

But hey, what does it know about meditation, or stress relief?

Absolutely nothing.

7

No Mistakes

This might be my favorite Miles Davis story ever.

Herbie Hancock was playing keyboard in an all-star band Miles was fronting. It was a night when the musicians were tight and the music was "on."

And in the middle of one of Miles's amazing solos, Herbie played a chord that he said, "Sounded completely wrong . . . like a big mistake."

And he recoiled from the mistake, pulling his hands off the keyboard and clutching the sides of his head.

It was that bad.

But Miles simply paused for a moment, and then played some notes that made the wrong chord right.

Herbie was so blown away that he simply couldn't play, couldn't even touch the piano, for a full minute. He just sat there, awestruck by the power of Miles's improvisational artistry.

Later he realized that Miles hadn't heard the chord as a mistake, he simply heard it as an event, as something that happened. And as the leader of a jazz band it was his job to respond to it, to improvise accordingly.

Herbie felt that the incident, which happened pretty early in his career, taught him a big lesson, not just about music, but about life.

> *We can look for the world to be as we would like it to be . . . But I think the important thing is that we grow, and the only way we can grow is to have a mind that is open enough to be able to experience situations as they are . . . to take poison and turn it into medicine . . . to take whatever situation you have and make something constructive happen with it.*
> — Herbie Hancock

Ain't that the truth?

I think I've done a pretty good job of paraphrasing, but you should go to YouTube and search for "Miles Davis according to Herbie Hancock" to hear him tell the full story.

8

Footsteps

The other morning I was walking our dog on the beach, barefoot.

It's a popular spot, so there were lots of footprints in the hard-packed sand close to the water's edge.

One set was from another pair of bare feet, about my size. So I started placing my feet where theirs had landed, matching stride for stride.

It was fun for a while. That aphorism, "Never judge someone until you've walked a mile in their shoes," popped into my head. But after about only twenty steps, I realized that their gait was just different enough from mine (left foot too turned out), that it started to feel awkward. I felt a little twinge in my hip, so I switched to another set of footprints.

Bigger feet, running shoes.

I had to lengthen my stride, picking up the pace.

Same result.

And then it hit me . . . how much of life is like that?

We start out following the paths laid down by others, because it's a good way to learn and to avoid mistakes.

But often we continue, following in someone else's footsteps, long past the point where it starts to feel uncomfortable, because we're told it's the right thing to do, because "everyone does it this way."

This dynamic applies to pretty much everything: career, relationships, parenting, fashion, music . . . even teaching meditation.

Stepping out on your own can feel awkward, even scary. You risk being criticized, even shunned, by people dismissive of your choices.

But it's the only way you'll ever hit your stride.

9

The Happiest
Accountant Ever

Years ago I had the pleasure of working with the most effusively happy accountant I've ever met. He was always smiling and laughing . . . and this was *during* tax-time.

I enjoyed my brief interactions with him so much that I offered to take him to lunch after tax season wrapped up.

He happily accepted.

But over lunch I learned that he had not always been so happy. That before he was an accountant he had been a tortured art student.

Huh?

He explained that he had been raised by a poet and a painter, with the expectation that he, too, would be a great artist.

But despite their insistent encouragement, despite having some skill with brushes and charcoals from years of classes and private tutoring, deep down he suspected that he was *not* an artist.

At the start of his senior year of high school, the dinnertime conversations revolved around what prestigious art school he would attend. Maybe SCAD, the Savannah College of Art and

Design? Or RISD, another top-tier school in Rhode Island? Or would he stay closer to home and go to Art Center, or Cal Arts? His parents were bubbling with anticipation.

One night he rather timidly suggested that he might take a gap year before diving into art school . . . maybe take a few business classes at community college?

His parents were dumbstruck.

"What? No . . . you don't want to be the man, a businessman . . . you're going to be a great artist," his dad said.

"You're going to blow us away," his mom beamed. "We can't wait to see what you do."

And so he was shipped off to art school, where he sucked at art, hated it, felt like a failure, started drinking heavily, became an alcoholic, and almost died late one night when he drunkenly drove his car into the trunk of a big tree on campus.

Turns out he hit more than the tree that night—he hit bottom. And, in the clarity that the bottoming-out experience can sometimes grace us with, he told his parents, with a certainty they couldn't brush away, that he wasn't an artist, that he loved numbers, and that he was going to business school.

This time they didn't try to talk him out of it.

His story seems unusual, but really it's the same old story we hear about all the time, just in reverse. Usually it's parents encouraging their kids to pursue more responsible careers, shooing them away from the arts.

I see it as a story of Push vs. Pull.

We live in a push culture. We mostly push our kids and ourselves onto paths that we think make sense, where we can earn a living, to make the safe, practical choice. And if we don't happen to love (or even like) what we do . . . well, that's why they call it work, right?

On a day-to-day basis we push our mind around constantly, telling it what to focus on, what to think about, what not to think about. We believe our best life is waiting to be lived if we could just get organized, steel ourselves with discipline and hard work, and finally push past all those nagging distractions that block us from achieving our—or maybe our parents'—dreams.

And yet we all feel a pull from somewhere deep within.

Maybe it's the pull to do something else, even if it's not the next logical step on our current career path, even if it's to do something totally different, something that wouldn't make as much money. Maybe it's the pull to start a new hobby, or maybe to do nothing at all and not feel guilty about it. Maybe it's the pull that leads us onto the path of enlightenment, whatever that might be. Heck, maybe just hearing the word "enlightenment" tugs at something deep within that doesn't care about where we are in our career or how our stock portfolio is doing.

As individuals, and as a society, I think we would benefit from more pull—to spend a little more time doing what we feel drawn to do, even if it has no practical benefit, especially if it doesn't make sense.

And I speak from experience. Almost 20 years ago, I was cleaning one of my bikes and heard a little voice within say, "You should be a meditation teacher."

It was so ridiculous I laughed out loud. I had a successful career in advertising. I made a lot of money. I was happy-ish.

I told my wife and she laughed too.

But that little voice kept tapping lightly at the edge of my awareness, and because I'd been meditating for a while—because

I had a daily experience of the inner silence from which that voice arises—I heard it. And one day I took the first, tentative step in the direction of that pull. I called my teacher and said that I'd been getting these weird thoughts about becoming a teacher myself. He said, "Yep, I was expecting this call . . . about 6 months ago."

What's that inner voice telling you?

Can you tune yourself to hear it, maybe just a bit better?

I wonder what would happen if you allowed yourself to listen?

Onto what happier, more deeply rewarding path would it offer to pull you?

10

You Can't Be Serious

Angels fly because they take themselves lightly.
— G.K. Chesterton

I felt like an imposter for the first year or so that I was teaching meditation.

I met other teachers who carried themselves with a kind of elegant reserve, detached, like they were holding back deep, spiritual secrets.

And although I was brimming with knowledge, and felt a calling to teach, I was still the same fast-talking, joke-cracking, irreverent guy I'd been when I was a creative director in advertising. Those traits paid off big in that business, but now I was . . . a meditation teacher?

I thought I should at least attempt to play the part.

So I went out and bought a long, flowing white caftan and some beads.

Really.

I wore that outfit a couple of times when teaching workshops, trying to cultivate a very "spiritual vibe," taking in a very measured way, with long pauses I hoped were pregnant with implied wisdom.

But I felt like an idiot, and realized that if I took myself so seriously I would have zero fun. And if I couldn't have fun teaching, then what was the point?

I went back to being the same fast-talking, joke-cracking, often irreverent me . . . with a sprinkling of profanity.

I've met plenty of people who liked what I had to say but felt that I wasn't "spiritual enough."

But for those I do click with? Well, the classes are full of laughter . . . and somehow people still learn how to meditate.

As the wonderfully silly Dr. Seuss once said, "No one is youer than you."

So be unabashedly, sincerely you in whatever you do.

All the other roles are already taken.

For a much deeper dive into this question of what role we're playing check out #45— Behind the Mask

11

The Myth of
Self-Improvement

A while back an old friend from my advertising days asked, "How's the self-improvement business?"

"It's going well," I said.

But what I didn't say is that I find the term misleading. Because really, there's no such thing as self-improvement.

Ask yourself, when a flower blooms, is it "improving itself?"

Is the bloom better than the bud?

Maybe to the florist, but certainly not to the flower.

No, the flower isn't improving itself. It's evolving. Progressing naturally from one stage to another.

All of nature is evolving. From the Vedic perspective, that's all nature knows how to do, and that's all it has been doing, from the Big Bang to this exact moment.

You are part of nature. Which means you're evolving.

From wherever you are now to whatever comes next.

There may be times when—to your ego, or your parents, or your peers—it might look like you blew it, that you're backsliding, or that you're stuck. Not advancing as quickly as you should. Not climbing to the next rung on your career ladder, or getting that advanced degree, or getting married, or buying a house, or having kids, or whatever it is you should have done by now.

But nature knows better.

Wherever you are now is *exactly* where you're supposed to be. And you're going in the right direction.

Sometimes it can be hard to remember that, and even harder to believe.

If you sometimes feel bad about being stuck check out #44—Three Steps Back.

Which is why I'm reminding you.

12

Flipped Off By a 4-Year-Old

The other day I was flipped off by a little boy. But he had a pretty good excuse . . . his mom did it first.

I was riding my bicycle through The Presidio, an old military base near the Golden Gate Bridge. The roads there are very curvy, and suddenly I found a minivan drifting into the bike lane. I swerved to the side and screamed, "HEY! WATCH IT!" or something less polite, but equally urgent. The driver jerked back into her lane, zoomed ahead and . . . flipped me off.

But this is San Francisco, so in a few blocks of heavy traffic I easily caught up with them.

And as I slowly pulled up alongside, this super-cute little boy in a car seat flipped me the bird.

It was appallingly adorable.

His mother sat there gripping the wheel, stone-faced, and wouldn't even glance at me.

Why did this happen? Because she's a terrible person? No, probably not. It's because her tank was empty. Not her gas tank, but her tank of what stress researcher Hans Selye called *adaptation energy*. This is the energy we use to deal with the demands of life. And Selye said that when our tank is full we can meet those demands with equanimity, with creativity, with perspective, or perhaps even a gracious, "My bad."

But when our tank is empty? When we're fried, frazzled and stressed out? In those situations, Selye said, we simply don't have the capacity to *interact* with life, so we're more likely to *overreact*, to shift into fight-or-flight mode.

So instead of apologizing to the cyclist we almost hit, we treat them like an enemy. And our kid learns an embarrassing lesson.

To put it another way, stress makes good people do bad things.

So what does this have to do with you?

When was the last time you ran out of gas in your car? I'm guessing never, or years ago . . . because most people regularly fill up their tank, and because a helpful little red light appears on the dash when you're running low.

But when was the last time you lost your shit? When you had a reaction to some ordinary life situation that wasn't, shall we say, representative of your best self?

I'm guessing more recently. Both because we're often stressed out, and because our internal dashboard doesn't have the same kind of early-warning indicators to show us we're running low on adaptation energy. (Wouldn't that be nice?) In fact, all too often it's embarrassing scenes like the one above that tell us we're in the red.

This is one of the biggest reasons I meditate, twice a day. To replenish my banks of adaptation energy. So that I can better handle the demands of life here in the big city with its congested traffic and distracted, burnt-out drivers.

So that instead of fight-or-flight, I can stay-and-play.

And so that my middle finger can remain where it belongs—wrapped around my handlebars.

I'm not perfect, nobody is, but I'm way better than before.

It's a nicer way to be in the world.

13

Go to Sausalito

I once gave a workshop in which I talked about meditation as a way to tap into an inner navigational beacon, something that's meant to guide us through life, something more dependable than the intellect, which is a fantastic tool but can be a *terrible* navigator.

Someone asked if I could give them a real-life example of this "inner navigational beacon" in action.

As it turns out, yes, I could.

It's a two-part story, and it's a true story, and it ends with a baby.

Part 1—India
The story begins in the springtime of 2011, high up in the foothills of the Himalayas, where I was in the middle of a three-and-a-half-month immersion training program to become a Vedic meditation teacher. Our little group was in the forest, far from any village, staying in this freezing, drafty and dilapidated old farmhouse, filled with giant spiders and surrounded by packs of howling red-faced monkeys. And we were doing all these crazy things like meditating 14 hours a day, trying to learn deep spiritual principles about the nature of consciousness, and memorizing a bunch of complicated rituals in Sanskrit, and everything else we needed to know to teach

people how to meditate . . . all while having to defend our kitchen from daily attacks by the monkeys and an angry, marauding cow that kept trying to break in to steal our vegetables.

And in the midst of all this chaos, one day I got a message brought up by a driver from the local village that my wife needed to talk to me about something very important. Which of course, made me freak out a bit.

I had an Indian cellphone which I hadn't used in a month because the service in the mountains was so terrible, but there was this one spot I could walk to about a mile away from our farmhouse where I could get within range of a cell tower that was on top of a mountain to make a call.

So that night I walked through the forest to where I could make a call, and she answered . . . and seemed happy to hear from me . . . so I thought, "Cool, she's not serving me with divorce papers."

She said, "We got a call on our Dear Birthmother letter."

Now, for those who don't know, my wife and I have two beautiful adopted boys, but at that time we had only one of them, he was 4 years old, and we'd decided we wanted to expand our family, to try again, so we'd had the adoption agency put our Dear Birthmother letter in circulation.

My wife and I had chosen what's called open adoption, and in that in that type of adoption prospective parents put together a letter that gets sent to prospective birth moms. Our was basically an ad: a 4-page brochure with a nice picture of our family, separate pictures of me, my wife, our son, and our dog, plus a little about what we do for work, why we love being parents, why we want to adopt again . . . all that stuff.

Another, more crude way of looking at it, was that our Dear Birthmother was a lure. We were fishing for a baby, and we had just gotten a bite.

A couple had seen our letter, liked it, and called my wife. The call went really well, and so she realized she needed to call me, to decide what we wanted to do. Because the baby was due in a month . . . and I still had almost 2 months of training to go. I wanted to be a meditation teacher. And we wanted to adopt a baby. But at that moment, it had to be one or the other.

And so over the course of the next few days we had a lot of calls back and forth . . . and I even got a chance to talk to the birth father, who was a very smart, funny and sincere guy.

It was a huge decision. And on the third night I asked my wife a question, the same question that had popped up in one of my morning meditations. It wasn't the kind of question you could really think too much about, or put together a pro/con list to help you come to the right decision.

I asked, "Does it feel like our baby?"

She paused, for just a bit, and then said, "No." Which is the same answer I'd come to. And so we passed on the opportunity . . . and we took our Dear Birthmother letter out of circulation until after I finished teacher training.

I also put a note in my calendar to reach back out to the birth father in a month, around the time the baby was due.

30 days later, I sent him a text that said something like, "Hey . . . I know you're on the cusp of a big decision. Just try to feel into it and you won't make the wrong one." I got a text back in 2 minutes, along with a lovely picture of mom, dad and the baby. "Her name is Samara, and we're keeping her! We love you!"

Part 2—Sausalito

So I finished the teacher training, came back to San Francisco, and started teaching. We also put our birthmother letter back into the mix, wondering . . . would we get another bite, or had we missed the opportunity?

And I started riding my bike again, something I'd really missed while in India. One morning in early fall, I hopped on and headed across the Golden Gate Bridge, and rode up into the Marin Headlands. I was thrashing myself up and down the hills, just loving it. I stopped to stretch at the top of Hawk Hill and realized I was STARVING, then realized I hadn't brought any snacks.

Every fiber of my being wanted to go to this new hoity-toity cycle café by this high-end British cycle wear company that had opened in the city while I was in India. And so that's where I wanted to go. I thought I'd get something to eat and then probably buy something, an expensive new jersey, or gloves, or a pair of socks . . . something I wanted, but definitely did not need. And my ego was getting all puffed up, thinking how good I would look in whatever it was I would buy . . .

And then this little voice popped into my head, a ping from that internal navigational beacon.

"Go to Sausalito."

But . . . that was the wrong direction. There was no fancy bicycle cafe in Sausalito. I couldn't spend too much on yet another unneeded jersey or jacket or gloves in Sausalito.

As I could feel the ego's insistent voice spinning up, I took a deep breath and let it out slowly. And in the natural space of calm and quiet at the bottom of the exhale I could feel, more than I could hear, the lingering echo of that inner voice.

Ping. "Go to Sausalito."

So I did. I rode away from the cycle cafe and towards what . . .
I wasn't sure. I found my way to a cafe overlooking the bay that
I knew had good food, and as I was parking my bike, I saw an
African-American woman with an adorable 3-year-old boy on her
lap, with these beautiful locks, chatting with one of her girlfriends.

I approached and said, "Hi, excuse me, my name is James, and this
might be an awkward question, but what product do you use in
your son's hair? I ask because I have an African-American son about
the same age, and we used to have his hair twisted in locks but they
got all ratty and smelly, so we shaved them off. But now we want
to start them up again and we're white and don't really know that
much about the process."

And she looked at me with this very odd expression and said, "I
know you. Well, I don't know you but I saw you and your wife and
son about three weeks ago at the food trucks in Larkspur Landing."

Huh. What a funny coincidence. I sat down and we started talking.
(After a few minutes I remembered that I had seen her and her
friend and her son there too, but hadn't said anything.) We talked
about parenting rambunctious little boys, about haircare, and a
bunch of other stuff until I heard my belly grumble, more loudly
this time. So I said goodbye and went inside to order.

When my number was called I grabbed the tray and started looking
for a place to sit.

Ping. "Go talk to her," came the impulse from within.

I resisted. I'd already been talking to her. I tend to be a pushy
person and often have to remind myself to give people their space.

"Go talk to her."

So I did. I went back out and made up some lame excuse about wanting to sit in the sun even though I was already fried from the long ride, because I never wear sunscreen no matter how many times my wife nags me to put it on.

They invited me to sit, and our conversation continued. But now we started talking about adoption, about why my wife and I decided to take that path to parenting, about what it was like being white parents with a beautiful chocolate-brown boy, how we chose open adoption so that we could have a relationship with his birth family. And I told her that we were looking to adopt again.

She looked at me with a quiet intensity I'll never forget and said, "I'm 8 months pregnant and have been thinking about placing the baby for adoption."

Oh . . .

So we all got this very tingly feeling, and I got her number, and her friend's number, and texted them both the name and number of our adoption agency. I told her that they'd send her a big stack of Dear Birthmother letters, and that there were a lot of families looking to adopt, not just us, and that she should go through them and see which ones resonated.

And then we stood up and hugged, and we agreed to all meet again next weekend for her son's 3rd birthday so that I could bring my wife and son to meet them. And then I watched as they drove away, waving.

And then I immediately called my wife and said, "I think I just met our birth mom."

She said, "What are you talking about?"

I said, "On my bike ride."

She said, "She was riding a bike?"

"No," I said, "She was definitely not riding a bike."

Long story short, she reached to the adoption agency and requested only our letter. We met again at her son's birthday party and agreed to move forward with the adoption paperwork.

About a month later, our second son, Joshua, was born. My wife and I were in the delivery room as he came into the world and into our life.

Epilogue

A couple weeks later we were visiting Joshua's birth mom, and she said that when she saw us that first night at the food trucks in Larkspur that she'd told her friend, "That's the family I want to place the baby with."

But, understandably, she didn't know how to break that ice.

"Hey, I see you've got a black kid already, and if you want another one I could hook that up for you . . ." isn't the kind of thing that falls easily off the tongue.

So when I walked up to them at the café that day they were stunned. And when I left to get my food they freaked out. "That's the guy!" "What do we do?" "Should I go talk to him?"

Then I walked back out, still following the guidance of that inner navigational beacon.

I think we all have that inner voice. We might call it intuition, or God, or divine providence or . . . it doesn't matter what we call it, as long as we can hear and honor it.

But usually we can't hear it because it's drowned out by the distortion of stress and all our incessant brain chatter. Or, if we do manage to hear it, we often argue with what it's telling us.

I think a daily meditation practice can help keep that line of communication open, even increasing the bandwidth a bit, and can give us the confidence to trust in the guidance we might receive even, and perhaps especially, when it runs counter to what the ego—out of fear or pride or whatever—tells us to do instead.

So, go to Sausalito. Or wherever that inner voice nudges you.

You never know what might happen.

Which is the point, really.

14

Reality, Augmented

With the metaverse all in the news, there's quite a bit of buzz about how future technology will allow us to be fully immersed in what is promised to be an augmented reality.

I'm no Luddite, but there's a pretty easy way to augment your experience of reality that doesn't require you to buy any more gizmos, and you certainly don't need to wait.

Try this simple exercise the next time you find yourself reflexively diving into your phone while waiting in line, eating, or just walking down the street.

1. Look up from your screen.

2. Look around.

3. Catch someone's eye and smile.
   (*Pro tip: it might be someone you're with.*)

4. Nod and/or say hi.

5. Watch them smile/nod/acknowledge.

6. If appropriate, engage them in conversation. Even small talk is fine.

7. Repeat.

Alternate exercise, if no people are nearby:

1. Look up from your screen.

2. Look around.

3. Or close your eyes and open your ears to the sounds swirling around you.

4. Repeat.

Just like that, your reality has been augmented.

And it won't cost you a dime.

My editor points out the Luddites weren't actually anti-technology. Google a Smithsonian article titled "What the Luddites Really Fought Against" to learn the truth about this very misrepresented movement.

15

On Becoming Unoffendable

You talking to me?
— Travis Bickle, from the film Taxi Driver

I used to leap at the opportunity to be offended.

And after being offended, sometimes long after, I would rehash the incident in my head, wishing I'd said this or that, or recalling with satisfaction some zinger I got in.

I would even invent whole confrontations in my head, rehearsing how it would go, and get myself all stirred up that way.

I was that guy.

Perhaps you know someone who fits the description. Perhaps, at times, you fit the description.

We live in a society where people are eager to take offense, to feel attacked, and then to attack back because, you know, "I was just defending myself." And social media comment threads are just making it worse.

After I started meditating every day (it helped to find an easy practice I could stick with), I started noticing something curious: it was getting harder and harder for me to feel offended.

I spent way less time arguing with people, both face-to-face and in my head.

And now I'm pretty much unoffendable. (Note: I did say "pretty much.")

Why?

Because meditation helped ground my identity in a direct experience of what I call the "essential self." Meaning that layer of self that lies underneath all the labels I tag myself with— parent, teacher, liberal, and so on. And that foundational layer of self can't be touched or tarnished by the opinions or actions of others.

And it certainly can't be offended.

And being grounded in that deep, inner self means that if you get in my face and criticize some aspect of me (my parenting, for example, or maybe my writing . . . I do tend to ramble on) I know that the real me, the whole me, isn't being attacked. So I don't have to get back in your face and get all defensive. So I can listen and learn.

Who knows, you might be right. Perhaps I could do something better. And if you're wrong? Well, often when people are critical, or angry at us, it actually says a lot more about them than it does about us . . . but if we're arguing we miss the opportunity to take in that useful information.

Being unoffendable doesn't mean that I don't still have issues and obstacles to overcome in my dealings with others. It's just that I manage to do so without as much rancor, and without bruising as many egos. Especially mine.

You got a problem with that?
— the author

*Check out #35—
1800 Years B.F.
(Before Facebook)
to see how ancient
wisdom can help
us better navigate
modern life.*

16

The Woo Line

I used to be a militant atheist. As a soon-to-be-ex-girlfriend once put it, listing off her reasons for dumping me, "You're one of the least-spiritual people I've ever met."

I was definitely not what you'd call a woo-woo kind of guy . . . not even semi-woo.

Now I teach meditation.

So what I call my Woo Line has moved quite a bit over the years.

The Woo Line is a concept I came up with one weekend when I was teaching meditation at Wanderlust, a massive, multi-day Yoga + Wellness festival in Squaw Valley.

One day, between workshops, I was hanging out backstage in the presenters' lounge between, sipping some tea and reading a book, when I heard a couple of women talking and decided to tune in to the conversation. Full disclosure: I LOVE eavesdropping; it's one of my sneaky, guilty pleasures.

One of the women asked, "So how's it going with you and Brad?"

Big sigh . . .

The other woman leaned in, sensing something juicy.

"Well," she said, "we're doing OK . . . but our spirit animals are fighting."

Wow . . . that's a tough one. But, I wondered, how would she know? And how could she and Brad get past it? Are there spirit animal reconciliation counselors who can help ease tensions between the badger and the owl?

I realized that the whole situation she was describing was well on the other side of my Woo Line. The line had moved a lot since my atheist days, but I was still, in comparison, what you might call semi-woo. And that's OK.

Now I'm not saying those women were wrong. I may, to be honest, have snickered a bit inside, but I've learned enough over the years, and had enough mind-blowing experiences, to know that my ego is not the final arbiter of what is and what is not possible. Shamans? Astral projection? Spirit animal squabbles as the source of relationship troubles? Just because I haven't experienced it doesn't mean it's not possible.

I don't know where your Woo Line is at present. And I don't really think it matters.

I think what matters is that it *moves.*

Little kids live in a magical, mysterious world of total woo . . . but it fades, the line moves, and that's not a bad thing. A 15-year-old who still believes in the magic of Santa is, well, a bit awkward. But as we move through our teens, 20s, and 30s, we start to construct a worldview that seems stable, held together with logic and science and a certain hard-boiled rationalism, and that's good too.

But if we're lucky, as we get older we find ourselves in situations in which the old answers don't satisfy. Cracks begin to show in the armor of our certainty. We start to question things, to consider things, to be open to ideas and practices and experiences that conflict with who we think we are.

That's how our Woo Line moves. That's how we grow.

> *The most beautiful thing we can experience is the mysterious. It is the source of all true art and all science. He to whom this 'emotion' is a stranger, who can no longer pause to wonder, or stand rapt in awe, is as good as dead. His eyes are closed.*
> — Albert Einstein

Turns out old Albert, like most theoretical physicists I've studied, was pretty woo himself.

17

Picking Up Other Dog's Poop

I'm a conscientious urban dog owner, which means I pick up our dog's poop . . . but not 100% of the time, because I walk him mostly in off-leash areas and sometimes he runs off and does his business out of sight.

A few years ago, I also started picking up after other people's dogs, and now I do it pretty much every time I take ours for a walk.

Why?

To be honest, I started doing it to shame a woman who stood there, watching and chatting on the phone and pretending not to notice while her dog took a huge dump right in front of her and, when he was done, she just kind of started to shuffle off, leaving the steaming pile behind. I was walking up the trail towards them, and as my dog started to nose around hers, I briskly whipped another biodegradable bag out of my pocket, looked her right in the eye and said, with a sneer and a fake smile, "That's OK, I've got it."

She had no reaction.

So I walked on, feeling smugly superior, with my dog bounding alongside, and then spotted another pile of poop, with no culprit in sight, and picked that up too . . . even though there was no one around to witness my good deed.

And I've been doing it ever since. Sometimes the other dog owner is nearby, pretending they don't see, but usually it's just poop that for whatever reason got missed. And if I have an extra bag handy I stoop down and pick it up. Sometimes I end up picking up four or five extra poops on a walk.

Why?

Well, I no longer do it to shame anyone. Or to feel better about myself. Although I'm certainly not immune to the compliments I sometimes get from passersby who notice what I'm doing.

I do it because nobody likes stepping in dog poop.

I do it because it's just become what I do.

But I've come to realize that the biggest reason is because I feel a sense of responsibility.

It's not my dog . . . but it's my dog park.

It's my city.

It's my world.

I pick up other dogs' poop because it feels good to do it . . . in a warm, squishy kind of way.

So why have I chosen to write about it?

I guess because I think there are thousands of small things we could all do.

Sometimes they're icky, but they're almost always easy.

Pick up a piece of trash off the sidewalk and carry it until you find a bin.

And guys . . . grab a wad of toilet paper and wipe the pee, even if it's not yours, from public toilet seats. (Yes, I do this too.)

Invite someone to share your table at the café, especially if it's a 4-top, even if you've already got your stuff spread out just how you like it. Don't pretend you don't see them scanning for a place to sit. I met one of my best friends this way.

Let someone merge in front of you, even if it means they make the light and you miss it. (74% of rush-hour accidents happen on the yellow, within 150 feet of the intersection.)

These are the right things to do.

They all make the world just a little bit better.

And the best part is that you'll feel better by doing them, once you let go of the idea that you're being inconvenienced.

The trick is to do whatever you do lovingly, not begrudgingly, the same way you'd reach across the table and gently wipe a smudge of ketchup off a little kid's cheek.

18

Who Ordered the Extra Serving of Drama?

I have a friend who will tell you how having a heart attack was a blessing in disguise. Because it allowed him to break from the life that led to that trauma.

You probably know someone who's experienced something similar—getting fired, having an affair, hitting bottom—or perhaps you can point to some terrible thing in your own life that now you can, with a wry laugh, admit was actually a good thing.

Have you ever wondered why this is such a common story? I mean, beyond the people-are-sometimes-stupid explanation?

The Veda has a better explanation. From the Vedic perspective, life is not a struggle between Good and Evil. Rather, there are three forces which govern the flow of evolution: Creation, Maintenance, and Destruction. And they're meant to be arranged in that sequence.

But we live in a society that puts Maintenance first. We're taught to hold on to things that are no longer working. To not make a move until we are certain that what's next will be better.

And so what happens is that we move along a path that we know is unsustainable. We know a job is killing us, but we keep at it because we're afraid to try something new. We fight the good fight in trying to make a failing relationship work and end up being embittered and angry.

And when Maintenance is first, Destruction is next in line, followed by Creation. It's why there are so many stories that go like this: "The worst thing that ever happened to me was the best thing that ever happened to me." Because that destructive event cleared away old irrelevancies, creating space for something new and more life-sustaining to sprout.

There are a lot of people who know, like my friend did, that they're on an unsustainable path. It might be in their career, or their relationship, or they might be living in a way they know is unhealthy for them.

I tell them there are two ways to get off an unsustainable path:

1) **You can step off.**

Stop putting all your energy into the path you're on. Don't just put your head down and plow ahead. Find another path and begin taking your first small steps. It doesn't have to make sense. When Steve Jobs flunked out of college he took a calligraphy class. Can you imagine what his parents thought? "What's that going to do for you?" But he fell in love with typography, and so when the Mac was introduced it was the first computer with proportionally spaced fonts. Who could've predicted? No one.

This option requires you to confront uncertainty . . . you probably won't know what's next. You'll have to adapt, to learn, to grow, and it might require you to take a few steps back from where you are now, which can seem like failure. This can be hard to do, especially when it comes to something like a career where most of us have

54

this crazy idea that we're supposed to be moving forward, making more money, climbing the next rung on the ladder ALL THE TIME.

2) Life will shove you.

Both are effective. One is way more drama.

Some people seem to require drama.

What about you?

I explore this idea of switching your life path in #30—Leaping. and The Proverbial Net and #52—Enthusiasm.

19

What's on Your To-Be List?

As I like to say, you're not a human doing, you're a human being.

Despite our obsession with productivity, biologists still haven't reclassified us as a species.

And yet for many of us, our sense of identity is totally tied up with what we do for a living. At a deep level we feel that our value as people is based on how much we get done, and if we do as good a job as possible.

So it's easy to fall into the busy trap, living as if life is one VERY long To-Do list. And at the end of the list there's a last item that just says DIE (and someone else has to check off that box for you), and then on your tombstone, or urn, or mushroom burial suit, they write:

SHE GOT IT ALL DONE

The mushroom suit is a real thing. Google it.

And everyone at the funeral thinks, "Wow . . . she did it! She got it all done. What a great life she must've had."

Which is ridiculous, because no one, including you, will ever get it all done. Because they would just give you more to do . . . or you, being the uber-achiever you are, would pile more onto your already full plate.

Now I'm not suggesting that you stop making To-Do lists, or use productivity apps or planners or whatever tool you find helpful.

I'm not saying that you should sit around and do nothing.

But I am suggesting that the true measure of how good a day you had isn't a long list chronicling all you got done, but what kind of person you were when immersed in all that doing.

Did you trample over others, or your best self, rushing and trying to cram everything into the dwindling hours of the day?

Or did you balance the desire to be as productive as possible with other, less quantifiable qualities?

So consider spending a few minutes today thinking about what and how you want to be in the world this week. (I like to use the time right after meditation for this.)

Do you want to be more loving, patient, curious, adventurous, supportive, kind, or . . . ?

Do you want to be a better listener, parent, friend, boss, spouse, or . . . ?

What qualities do you want to embody?

What roles do you want to shine in?

Write them down.

Make a To-Be list.

And then fill out your To-Do list in alignment with that.

Today I Would Like To Be:

_____

_____

_____

_____

_____

_____

_____

20

Gift Wrapping

I'm the person the gift bag was invented for, because I both dread and suck at wrapping gifts.

My wife, on the other hand, LOVES wrapping gifts. So around the holidays my job is to hold the tape, keep track of the scissors, and refill her eggnog.

If it were up to me (and, as long as I'm married, it's not), I would just give people gifts unwrapped.

And that got me thinking . . .

In my teaching I often reference one of Shakespeare's most-quoted lines from *Hamlet*:

> *There is nothing either good or bad, but thinking makes it so.*

Usually this is interpreted to mean that things are neither good nor bad . . . they just are. Which is absolutely true. And much suffering results from people labeling things they want to happen as good and things they wish didn't happen as bad.

But the idea can sometimes lead the spiritually lazy to adopt a passive, "Well then, since things are what they are and there's nothing I can do about it, I might as well just practice my Zen-like detachment."

But there's a much more active and engaged interpretation: that by *choosing to think differently* about a situation, we can transmute it from a horrible calamity to the proverbial golden opportunity. Or from a minor irritation to a smaller opportunity . . . like being stuck in holiday traffic means we get to listen to another episode of our favorite podcast.

We can see anything that happens as an unwrapped gift.

OK, so that sounds wise and all . . . but what does it really mean?

It means that, instead of throwing up our hands in despair when something "bad" happens, we challenge ourselves to do the work to find the opportunity, the "good," embedded in it.

We can ask ourselves, "What do I have to do so that, years from now, when I look back at the current horrible, effed-up situation, I can say, 'That was one of the best things that happened to me.'"

Now, I know that just changing our thinking isn't enough. But it's definitely the start that then leads to the actions we can take based on our reframing.

It's not easy, but it *is* a skill you can cultivate.

And I think that with everything unfolding in the world right now, it might be a good skill to consider honing.

21

Snarling Little Dogs

There's this house my son and I walk past on the way to the beach, and every time we get close these two tiny dogs rush the fence, barking and snarling with an intensity that would be terrifying if it weren't so ridiculously funny. They follow us all the way along the fence and don't stop barking until we're about 100 feet away.

And they do this every single time . . . and I'm sure to everyone who walks past.

"What do you think they're saying?" my son once asked.

"Oh, something like, 'Don't you dare come into our yard! If you even think about coming in here we'll rip your face off! Look at these teeth! Grrrr!'"

Toss in a few doggy f-bombs and I think that's pretty much it.

Usually I don't give them a thought—well, other than to think I'm glad they're not my dogs.

But my son asking me about what the dogs might be saying to us got me thinking about what they might turn and say to each other after someone walks past.

Maybe something like, "Good job. That worked. They didn't breach the perimeter. Keep it up."

So what's really happening here?

With their super-tuned senses, the dogs perceive a threat, race to the fence, act aggressively to repel the threat, feel validated when the threat doesn't materialize, and so continue to repeat the behavior.

But we were never a threat. We had no intention of going into their yard, and if they weren't barking so viciously, we might even bend down to pet their little heads or offer some tasty treats.

I think we all have a snarling little dog inside us.

A hyper-vigilant little beast, pricking up its ears at the tiniest sign of potential danger, lunging and snarling to protect us from non-existent threats. The irony is that in our desperate attempt to stay safe, we just end up hurting ourselves.

We pull back in relationships when we actually crave intimacy.

We take offense where none was intended—and even when someone *does* mean to offend us, we react as if our life is in danger, when really it's just our ego that gets bruised.

And so we defend our turf—not just our homes, but our inboxes, our beliefs, our roles at work, our opinions online, our timelines, our cultural traditions and norms. We plant little flags on territory that isn't under threat, and bark and snarl as if it is . . . and we get even more worked up when someone dares to question our right to be outraged.

And this is just in our day-to-day lives.

Sometimes the stakes are higher.

Think of the Christ archetype . . . and yes, I realize that some snarling dogs might start yapping just at the mention of Jesus. So don't think of the historical figure—that carpenter guy who may or may not have actually existed. Don't think of the religious symbol. Think of what Jesus represents: the liberator, the teacher of love, the one who sees clearly and invites others to drop their illusions, their false sense of separateness, and do the same.

Jesus challenged the authority of both religious leaders and Roman rulers—not because he came with weapons or armies, not by attacking them directly, but by embodying a radically different kind of authority: rooted in love, compassion, and a direct connection to the divine. Jesus was dangerous *not because he posed a military or political threat*, but because his presence *exposed the emptiness* of the systems they upheld and of the hollowness of the lives they were living.

This is what all great spiritual teachers, and teachings, do.

And so Pharisees barked.

The Romans snarled.

And in the end, they nailed him to a cross.

And then they erected a religion in his name that pretty much ignores his most challenging, and liberating, teachings.

Like when Jesus said, "The Kingdom of Heaven is spread out upon the Earth, but men do not see it." Meaning it's here, now, for everyone . . . not a place you go when you die if you're judged to be worthy or special.

Or the idea that a rich man has about as much chance of getting into Heaven as a camel does of passing through the eye of a needle . . . meaning none at all.

This last bit about the camel is particularly threatening to our current capitalist, materialist, consumer-based society in which we worship at the altar of the Almighty Economy and venerate billionaires as if they were saints to be emulated and admired. A culture in which even some churches preach what they call "the Prosperity Gospel," promising happiness and salvation can be ours if we just make enough money, and donate enough to the church, and spend enough to surround ourselves with all the Earthly things we want.

And on our deepest psychological and spiritual levels, the teachings of Christ, the Buddha, and other great sages don't just threaten our external institutions and deeply held beliefs—they threaten the ego itself.

Jesus spoke of dying to the self, of losing one's life to find it, of turning the other cheek and loving your enemy. "Meaning what?" we sputter. "That I'm supposed to love Donald Trump?"

Yeah, that's what it means, impossible as it seems.

Buddha teaches that all suffering is born of clinging to our stuff, to our ideas, even to our sense of being a separate, individual self.

The great Vedic sages teach that all of material existence is illusion, and must be dropped, must be seen through completely, for us to experience nirvana—the heaven, that is and can only be experienced here, now.

These teachings are *still* radical, are still threatening, thousands of years later, because they challenge us to drop our defenses, surrender control, and trust in something bigger than the little me we so desperately cling to.

For the ego—the ultimate snarling little dog—that kind of surrender *feels like death*. And so it resists, even violently.

So, what can we do?

Well, I think the first step is to take some time to reflect, to ask, without judgment, "What triggers my snarling little dog to leap into attack mode? What does it bark at?"

Think about it. And let me know what you come up with.

But then keep going. Ask yourself the deeper question:

"What might I experience—what might I finally see—if I got that damned dog to stop barking, and opened the gate?"

22

The World is for
Looking At

This morning I saw a pedestrian get hit by a car, in very slow motion, just around the corner from my meditation studio. He was bruised and scared, and then angry, but not (it appeared) seriously hurt.

The driver was profusely apologetic.

It could've been worse.

As you might guess, both the walker and the driver were staring at their phones when it happened.

I saw the whole thing . . . because I wasn't on my phone.

Now I'm not writing to say you shouldn't be glued to your phone when crossing the street, or when you're driving.

(But *of course* you shouldn't.)

The point I want to make is a bigger one.

Our phones are amazing. They play a huge role in our lives. I wouldn't want to be without mine.

But the world is bigger, and more amazing.

And the world is for looking at.

There is so much beauty, even on the grungiest block, if we would only allow ourselves to see.

So many faces we pass. Opportunities to share a smile, or to connect, if even for a moment, with someone who's suffering. So many homeless begging for a handout, but who really crave human connection—eye contact, to be seen as people, just a nod of the head, or maybe some small talk and a handshake—if we would only look up from our phones.

So many details, the ever-present play of light and shadow.

You can ALWAYS find something to see, even in the dreariest room, the dullest elevator, and seeing will keep you grounded in the present moment.

And being grounded in the present? That's kind of why we're here.

But I get it.

Reflexively diving into our screens is perhaps the most common way we deflect the anxiety that rushes in when our brains are idle.

We're a restless, over-scheduled society, and there's always something to check up or in on . . . so you don't miss out!

So you're as productive as possible!

And instead you miss out on the world around you. Which sometimes has cars and pedestrians in it.

So the next time you find yourself mindlessly diving into your phone . . . and you manage to catch yourself . . . stop, look up and look around. See what there is to see.

It's well worth the brief time it takes . . . and might just help extend the time you have.

23

Splish-Splash

You may have heard the old expression, "You never step in the same river twice." Because both you and the river are different each time.

And while that's empirically true on a molecular level, it's one of those phrases that can leave you scratching your head a bit, wondering what you might actually DO with this particular pearl of wisdom.

I think the thing to do is forget about rivers and think about relationships.

We all know that a first date is different than a third date.

But the longer you're together, there is a tendency to start taking things for granted, as if there's no difference anymore, you're just going through the motions, going to the same restaurants, sitting on the same sides of the couch to watch movies, laughing in the same way as you listen to your partner tell the same stories . . . and so on.

And while there's a certain undeniable comfort that can come from the well-worn grooves of a shared life, what was once a flowing river, a relationship that was "going somewhere," can now seem more like an eddy, off to the side, swirling in a lazy circle with some dead leaves and a water-logged stick.

I've been married to the same amazing woman for over 20 years. I get it.

But this apparent repetitive cycle of sameness is an illusion. It's just a habit of thought that coalesces into predictable patterns of action.

And because it's an illusion, it only has the weight you give it. Illusions endure as long as you believe in them, and as soon as you stop believing, even a little, they begin to dissolve.

So . . . what would it mean to embrace the truth that you never step in the same relationship twice? That neither you, nor your partner, are the same people you were yesterday, which means that your relationship, this living thing that you co-create in the space between the two of you, can be as fresh and vital as a river surging with spring snowmelt.

What would you do, could you do, differently?

Start today.

24

An Unfair Comparison

I remember the day I quit trying to meditate.

I was sitting in a Zen center, with my legs crossed uncomfortably underneath me, fighting the pain in my creaky knee, and trying to control my mind which was racing with thoughts about my girlfriend, who I was pretty sure was going to break up with me. (And I was right!)

I opened my eyes and looked at the other meditators and thought, "Oh my god . . . look at them. They're so calm. I'm a fraud. I can't meditate. I don't belong here."

And so I quit . . . and went almost 15 years before trying again.

Since becoming a meditation teacher I've come to realize that the reason I quit had very little to do with my racing mind. It was that I was comparing my inside experience with what I could see on the outside of the others around me. I looked at their serene faces and just *knew* they must be having a different, better, more "meditative" experience than I was.

But I was wrong.

Not only did I eventually discover I could meditate, but years of teaching have taught me that everyone has too many thoughts. That everyone struggles and wonders if they're doing it right. Comparing what was going on in my head with what I imagined was going on in their heads was an unfair comparison.

Unfortunately, it's a comparison we make often. Not just in Zen centers, but in everything.

We look at other people and make the ridiculous assumption that because they look really happy in that photo, or are driving that shiny new car, or because their kid got into that school, or because they're riding that fancy new carbon-fiber bike, that they must be *so happy*. (OK . . . maybe the last one is just me.)

At some level we know this isn't true. We know that everyone struggles with something, at least some of the time. But we rarely apply that insight to ourselves.

Look at it another way. Imagine someone came up to you and sheepishly admitted that, despite appearances, they were really struggling to hold it all together.

Would you sneer and call them a loser?

Tell them to suck it up and stop whining?

I'm guessing no.

So when you're the one who's having a hard time—whether that's in a meditation center, or at work, or in your relationships, or whatever—maybe think about treating yourself the way you'd treat them.

Nicely.

25

But Does it Scale?

There's this idea, very popular in Silicon Valley, that to have a real impact in the world you have to "affect the lives of a billion people."

Entrepreneurs and investors look for ideas that can scale. The ideas that do can end up being valued at billions of dollars.

But maybe the most truly valuable things are those that don't scale.

Let me give you an example.

On Saturday our family spent the day in the coastal town of Santa Cruz, mostly at the beach and the quaint amusement park on the boardwalk. We endured long lines for rickety rides, we ate all manner of sugary and fried foods, and my sons, after years of failing, finally defeated me in air hockey. It was loud. It was fun. It was filling.

It was e-x-h-a-u-s-t-i-n-g.

At 9:30pm, I left my wife and younger son, who were both wiped out, at a restaurant while my 16-year-old and I started hoofing it back up the long hill to where we parked the car . . . probably about a mile away.

It was dark, cloudy, with no moon. Coming down a steep section where the sidewalk narrowed, we saw a woman, wobbling behind a rickety aluminum walker. She looked to be in her 50s, shivering because her thin, short-sleeved shirt offered little protection from the wind whipping off the ocean.

My son Logan, who was in front, asked, "Are you OK?"

She stopped, looked up and said no. She was not doing OK. Not at all. And then she started crying.

In between sobs and broken speech, the effects of a recent stroke, we discovered that her name was Lisa, that she was lost, and that she didn't know how she was going to get somewhere safe to spend the night.

I gave her my jacket, and I told Logan to stay with her while I ran up the hill for the car. When I got back, we folded the walker and helped her into the front seat. I called my wife to tell her what was going on and that we'd be back as soon as we could.

Lisa told us she was trying to get to where her boyfriend's truck was parked, that her boyfriend had been arrested earlier that day, and that she hoped to sleep in the truck or in a friend's place nearby. It was near a care facility that was closed for the night, but where she could get the anti-stroke meditation she needed in the morning. We plugged that into Google Maps and discovered it was 4.7 hilly miles away—13 minutes by car but an impossible journey for a freezing, stroke-addled woman with a walker.

Can you imagine?

Long story short, we found the truck, found the friend's house, ignored the giant BEWARE OF DOG sign, opened the creaking gate, walked her up the rocky path, rang the bell and got her settled with her friend, a woman with a warm smile named Cory.

As we left, Lisa gave us both a tight, trembling hug, then turned to Logan, and said that lots of people had passed her on that narrow sidewalk, but that he was the only one that stopped to ask how she was doing.

"Thank you for noticing me," she said. "Thank you for caring."

That's what doesn't scale. Genuine human concern. Compassion in the moment, one person for another, and the willingness to act on it.

The stock market can't put a value on that.

You won't get a lot of venture-capital funding with a pitch deck that says "We're going to encourage people to notice, and go out of their way to help, random people they meet on the street."

You won't build an app that impacts a billion people.

But it had a hell of an impact on at least 3 people that night . . . and maybe, in the telling of the story, a few more.

And that's more than enough for me.

26

Falling Awake

I discovered insomnia in college. Not because I suffered from it, but because once I heard some people in my dorm talking about their struggles with insomnia, and I said, "Dude, I know what you mean . . . sometimes it can take me 15 to 20 minutes to fall asleep."

That, they assured me, with daggers in their eyes, was NOT insomnia, and could I please go fuck off.

Every girlfriend I've ever had, including the one who became my wife, has marveled at my ability to Just. Fall. Asleep.

They ask how I do it. And of course I can't tell them. Because I don't know. No one does.

Sleep isn't something you do, it's something that happens to you. That's why the verb is falling, not achieving, or accomplishing, or making sleep.

The longer I spend on a spiritual path, the more I've come to realize that the same principle applies with awakening, enlightenment, expansion of awareness . . . whatever you call it.

A lot of people want to know how. They want to know what they can do to make it happen, you know, faster if possible, although many are aware of the trap that wanting it to happen faster probably slows it down.

But neither I, nor any teacher, can tell you how.

And if you meet someone who promises they can, run.

Now, it's not totally random. Like with sleep, there are practices that make it more likely, that tilt us—sometimes slightly, sometimes steeply—in the right direction.

Meditation helps. Asking and contemplating deep questions. Reading and listening to spiritual stuff. Spending time in nature. Finding different ways to cultivate stillness.

But actual moments of awakening, of transcending, of experiencing oneness, whatever you call them, they just . . . happen.

And generally not when we're trying to make them happen.

We trip, accidentally, over our egoic defenses.

We fall awake.

It's a kind of grace. Something given, not earned.

27

After the Storm

I went for a walk after breakfast this morning and spent an hour sitting at the sea, watching waves pound the beach, something that's been happening for about a week now as the California coast has been awash with heavy rains and howling winds.

One of the most striking consequences of the recent slew of storms is that the beach is pretty much carpeted—and I mean wall-to-wall—with debris, including a staggering number of tree trunks, massive pieces of destroyed piers, whole telephone poles and even a giant shipping buoy.

In my many years of visiting Ocean Beach I've never seen anything even remotely like it.

And as I sat there watching the sea I noticed a huge tree trunk, must've been 20 feet long and 3 feet thick.

It started out stranded on the beach, got sucked out to sea, got tossed and tumbled in the waves and backwash, and finally, after about an hour of that, ended up back on the beach about 50 feet from where I first saw it.

All that tumult and no progress.

Life can be like that too.

Storms sweep in, and even the big, seemingly solid things we hoped we could count on get uprooted, and we're left feeling unmoored and adrift at the whim of forces much bigger than we could ever hope to contain.

Sometimes things just suck, and the lessons—the ones people like me are supposed to remind us to look for—seem a *long* way off.

In fact, sometimes the forecast calls for more storms.

And then as I was walking back, I noticed that someone, probably a group of someones, had used pieces of driftwood, some of them really big, to build a rudimentary shelter. It must've taken them hours, and I'm sure it won't be there tomorrow. The surging tide will sweep in and wipe it out.

But that's not the point.

The point, such as I took from it, is that the certainty we crave can't ever be found in the solid, heavy places we'd like to find it.

Much suffering is due to this misplaced hope.

But what is certain is that within us, both individually and collectively, is the impulse to clean up, to start again, to rebuild, to find some order in the chaos, ephemeral though it might be.

The certainty we seek in the world is actually something we bring to the world.

And I found some comfort in that.

28

Contagious

It was a VERY blustery San Francisco morning, and I was rushing to meet a friend for a coffee, hustling along a bustling street, when I turned the corner and almost slipped on a stack of those free newspapers that had been strewn in several big clumps across the sidewalk. Like someone had just opened the kiosks, grabbed all the papers, and angrily thrown them on the ground.

The wind had started to unravel the stacks, scattering sheets a good way down the block and into the street.

So I bent down, snatched up an armful, and started stuffing them into the trash can on the corner.

As I turned back to gather more, I saw a very posh, older woman crossing the street with a strange look on her face. Then she bent down, grabbed a bunch of papers, and smiled as she passed me on her way to the trash.

So now we were both cleaning up.

And then a cyclist dismounted, leaned his bike against a shop window, and started helping.

And then a homeless guy, who had the *brilliant* idea of putting the papers back into the kiosks, because the trash can was getting overfull.

And then a woman with her 7-year-old-ish kid who scampered like a happy puppy, having a blast.

No one said anything.

But everyone was smiling, happy to have contracted the helper virus.

And when all the papers were cleaned up, we all went on our way.

It made my day.

29

Balloons

As any young child can confirm, balloons are fun.

Fun to blow up, fun to bat around, fun to rub on the carpet and then stick to your hair.

But while balloons are certainly fun, at some point they're going to pop, and then the fun is over, and there might even be some tears.

"What happens," a kid at a birthday party once asked me, "to the air inside the balloon when it pops? Where does it go?"

I told him that nothing happens to the air inside the balloon. It doesn't go anywhere.

The thin film of stretched latex that held the air for a while, in that classic balloon shape, is torn and lying limp on the ground, or snagged in some prickly bush. But the air inside the balloon pretty much stays where it was, just remixing with the air that, only a moment before, was "outside."

I think this is an interesting way to think about death, which I know a lot of people would rather not think about.

Fear of death is the great fear, the primordial dread, the fear that drives so much of our relentless seeking, our bucket-list making, our overpriced, age-defying skin creams, and the fear nipping at the well-heeled heels of all those billionaires trying to hack immortality.

It's because we identify as the fragile balloon that's been stretched tight into the shape of our bodies, not as the life force, the consciousness, that has been breathed into it.

Meditation is good at allowing us glimpses of a transcendent truth: That we are not human beings having the occasional spiritual experience, we are spirit having the experience of being human.

We are the conscious life force power of the universe contained in these amazing, wonderful bodies.

We are here to have the full experience of what it is to be alive, all the highs and the lows, to get batted around for a while, no one ever knows for how long, and then . . . pop.

As the Buddhist saying goes, "Death is certain, the time is not. Knowing this, what is the most important thing now?"

I get that might seem morbid, especially for those who would rather think about anything but death.

But I think if we devoted a fraction of the energy spent denying and defying death into answering that question, day by day, it would be the most life-honoring thing we could do.

If you want to explore this topic a little more deeply skip over to #70—Kick the Bucket List.

30

On Leaping, and the Proverbial Net

Perhaps you've heard the expression, "Leap, and the net will appear."

It's often cited in those inspirational stories of someone who just went for it and succeeded beyond their wildest dreams. Sold all their stuff, quit their job, hit the road, maxed out their credit cards . . . you know, the kind of uplifting, the-universe-has-your-back kind of story that plays well on social media and in self-help circles.

And by all means, yay for those people.

But what about the rest of us?

People who maybe have others counting on them for food, shelter, care?

The ones who worry they might have too much at stake?

People too scared to leap?

There's a Spanish palindrome that provides a very practical, actionable answer. It may be the wisest palindrome ever.

La ruta nos aportó otro paso natural.

(Really, it reads the same backwards as forwards. So cool.)

Translation: "The path provides the natural next step."

Real-life translation: Don't put your head down and continue trudging along a path that you know, deep in your heart, isn't yours and might just be slowly crushing you.

Don't settle for a stagnant life.

You don't have to worship at the Altar of Inertia.

Lift your head up.

Look around.

And then take a step off the well-worn path of your life.

A small, tentative step in a new direction.

And then pause and look for the next step along this new, probably unpaved, path.

String a few of those together and pretty soon it will be as if you've leapt with both feet onto an entirely new path.

People (including, perhaps, you) will be amazed and wonder how you did it.

Student Driver

I was following behind a small knot of VERY slow-moving cars, and things were getting tense, horns were starting to blare, when the car at the head of the group made a slow, halting turn . . . and I saw the sign, STUDENT DRIVER.

And whatever irritation I was feeling popped like a bubble and I felt, if anything, sorry for the poor kid.

And then I thought, what if there were other signs? Signs that said things like . . .

BAD BREAKUP

JUST LOST MY JOB

WIFE DIAGNOSED WITH CANCER

MY KIDS ARE DRIVING ME CRAZY!

Or, and this might be the most common sign . . .

SORRY, BUT I'M REALLY, REALLY STRESSED OUT TODAY!!!

But there aren't signs like that. Which means we have to make them up for ourselves.

Which means that whenever we encounter someone, whether online or out in the real world, acting in ways we judge as insensitive or rude or just plain WRONG, we have a choice:

1. We can assume they're assholes, and honk, tweet, scream, shame, flame, or whatever.

2. We can imagine they're having a hard time, that they are students, learning some of life's hardest lessons, and give them a break.

Sounds good, right?

As it turns out I got a chance to try this out a couple miles later . . . and failed miserably.

I got stuck behind a car waiting to make a left turn on Van Ness Blvd, a street you haven't been able to turn left on for at least 20 years. Traffic was heavy, and there was no way to go around them before I missed yet another light.

I'll be honest, my first thought was, "What a jerk!" And as my mind was getting spun up I caught myself and thought, "Hmm . . . .what sign can I imagine hanging in their rear window? What story can I tell myself instead of sitting here seething with anger?"

Maybe they're a tourist and they're lost.

Maybe they're an old person, who probably shouldn't be driving, and honking at them will just make it worse.

Or maybe they just got a call that their kid is hurt, and they are simply taking the fastest, most direct route to wherever they need to be.

Now I want to be really clear—when we do this we are making up a story.

We don't have any idea if what we're coming up with to excuse or explain the offending behavior is true. But then we don't really know if the other story, the negative one, is true either.

And whether it's true or not isn't even the point. The point isn't what's happening in the outside world, it's what's happening inside us.

Because when we tell ourselves a story that gets us all riled up, unless we do something stupid to act on our anger, the person that's most affected is us.

Coming back to the story that started this post, I don't know if the people who were honking, and swearing, and flipping off the student driver ever even saw the sign hanging in the back window.

But I do know that what was coursing through their nervous systems—that caustic chemistry of anger and frustration—was very different from what was flowing through mine.

We tell ourselves stories all day. Why not tell nicer ones?

32

On the Inherent Interest of Twisty Paths

When we make plans we tend to think in straight lines. We'll do this, then that, then that, and by the time we're however many years into our career/life/relationship we'll be promoted to supervisor/own a home/have two kids . . . you know what I mean.

And a big, heaping bowl of suffering is served up when the course and timing of our life doesn't stick to the script.

But straight lines are boring.

Nobody listens to the scales as music—each note trudging along the predictable path, one after the other, with no surprising sharps or flats.

Yawn.

Nobody sits alongside an irrigation ditch to write poetry—too straight.

A river is better for that kind of thing because rivers bend.

We call curvy roads "the scenic route."

And when you read or listen to the life story of anyone interesting, what stands out are the curves, the unexpected twists and turns where life deviated, often sharply, and sometimes disastrously, from the linear naiveté of their carefully thought-out plans.

Look back at your own life and you'll probably see this is true for you too.

It's the curves that make life interesting.

But when we tell our stories we tend to avoid many of the curves, the twists in the path. Because often those are things we are too ashamed to admit even to ourselves, let alone anyone else.

But those are the things that make us human.

That make us relatable.

There is no better expression of this truth than Brené Brown's powerful TED talk on the power of vulnerability and how it's the gateway to deeper, more-intimate connections.

And in a world where so many feel isolated and lonely, what better tonic could there be?

But because we can hold onto the shame of those experiences for years, decades even, it can be difficult to allow ourselves to even think of them without cringing and wanting to hide. And to share them with others . . . with strangers? Forget about it.

I think the daily practice of meditation can help in two ways. First, by allowing us to decrease the level of irritation and agitation that stress creates. So we feel a little less raw, a little more of the time.

But more importantly, meditation is a way of connecting to the deeper place within us where there is no shame. Where we can know ourselves as beautiful and whole, not the flawed creatures stumbling through life that we might believe ourselves to be. And having an experience of that truth, day after day, changes us.

Almost 20 years ago I had an affair, which blew up in the ugliest, most soap-operatic way you can imagine.

It was terrible. Shameful. But it was the catalyst for my wife and me to start meditating. I used to be embarrassed about it. But now I see the affair as a giant boulder that was dumped into our path. A boulder that split us apart for a time. An obstacle that, like a river, we flowed around and past, and then, with a lot of love and the help of a great marriage counselor, the separated streams of our lives flowed back together.

I don't know what twist in your story meditation can help you own. But I do know that owning it, whether you choose to share it or not, can be a powerfully healing thing.

33

No One Completes You

The other morning my youngest son was sweetly singing the refrain that old song, *You Are My Sunshine,* where the singer goes on and on about how their beloved is the light of their life, is responsible for their happiness, and begs them not to take their sunshine away.

And as he was singing it, over and over and over and over (as kids do), it hit me that this song gets to the root of a very dangerous idea we have about relationships: that someone else can be our source of light. And that if they take that light away we will be cast into darkness and despair.

Let's examine this.

If I enter into a relationship hoping that you will fill me up with your light and make me whole, then I am defining myself as lacking. And so coming from that place of lack, I see you as necessary to "make me happy," as the song suggests. And if you're entering into our relationship with the same idea, then it will be my job to make you happy.

I can't quote the exact lyrics, because they are, believe it or not, still protected by copyright, but if you want to remind yourself of how cloyingly sweet a song it is just search YouTube for You Are My Sunshine.

It's easy to see how this will go.

We will both feel a rush of bliss-bunny fulfillment, with lots of sex and cuddling and sweet, romantic gifts in the early phase. But when that phase begins to wear off, as it tends to do, each of us will start noticing that familiar, nagging feeling that something is missing.

But . . . how could anything be missing if we complete each other, if we fill in all of each other's gaps?

So then I think, maybe you're not the right person. Maybe I need someone else to make me happy.

And the cycle repeats.

The truth is that no one can make us happy. No one will ever do all the right things, in exactly the right way, consistently enough and long enough. It's not only impossible, it's exhausting.

Ancient Vedic wisdom teaches that we are already whole. That our light shines, as does our happiness, from within.

Meditation gives us a way of connecting to this source. And when we can routinely cultivate the experience of our inner wholeness, we can begin to live from that place, and see that our job is to export the love that is our nature to the world, instead of chasing love in the world.

This is a radical way to live. One in which we don't place the absurd demand on any relationship to complete us. We understand that no one has our love locked up somewhere, and if we just act in the right way they will open the gates and love will flood into our lives.

When we are grounded in this wholeness, our relationships can become the playgrounds of our fulfillment, instead of the battlegrounds of our neediness.

34

Be Your Own Valentine

Compulsory romance has always been my least favorite kind, so I've never been a big Valentine's Day guy.

(Case in point, I'm writing this after returning from a lovely date with my wife . . . the night *before* Valentine's Day.)

And yet, beneath my crusty-curmudgeon exterior, there is a part of me that really loves the idea of a holiday on which you declare how you feel about a certain special someone.

But what if that special someone was you?

What if you could be your own Valentine?

I get that for most people it's easier to hand someone a fun, flirty card that says, "I love you," than it is to stand in the mirror, look deeply into your own eyes and say, "I love me."

Because no one is better at chronicling the long list of our unlovabilities than we are.

So how do you do it?

How do you be your own Valentine?

Here's a little thought experiment:

Imagine you walk out your front door and find a baby, lying in a basket. (Very biblical, I know, but stick with me.) It's crying, snot running down its nose, maybe even a bit stinky.

What would you do?

Well, you'd bend down right?

You'd pick that baby up and say, *There, there baby.*

It's OK, baby.
I'm here, baby.
I love you, baby.

Now, imagine that baby is you.

With all your flaws and faults.

All your soiled, stinky humanity.

All love is based in self-love.

So love yourself.

35

1800 Years B.F. (Before Facebook)

I was watching a comment thread unfold the other day, with insults flying back and forth, the vitriol rising higher and higher, when this quote leapt out from the background of my memory.

> *Choose not to be harmed, and you won't feel harmed. Don't feel harmed, and you haven't been.*
> — Marcus Aurelius, *Meditations*

So I posted it on the thread, as a way of trying to help someone understand that they had a choice not to be offended . . . and of course I ended up offending them.

Live and learn.

Which was pretty much the motto of Marcus's life, which he chronicled in his timeless collection, *Meditations*.

There are a lot of good translations of Meditations. My favorite is the Gregory Hays' from 2003

The book is full of wisdom that's as applicable today as it was almost 2,000 years ago. But perhaps the most inspiring thing about the book is that Marcus never meant for his meditations to be read by anyone.

It was more like a journal, a series of notes he wrote to himself, because he needed to be reminded of the principles by which he wanted to live.

This bit about having to rouse himself out of his morning lethargy is a great example of what I'm talking about.

> At dawn, when you have trouble getting out of bed, tell yourself: I have to go to work—as a human being. What do I have to complain of, if I'm going to do what I was born for—the things I was brought into the world to do? Or is this what I was created for? To huddle under the blankets and stay warm?

> So you were born to feel nice? Instead of doing things and experiencing them? Don't you see the plants, the birds, the ants and spiders and bees going about their individual tasks, putting the world in order, as best they can? And you're not willing to do your job as a human being? Why aren't you running to do what your nature demands?

Had there been something called the snooze bar in ancient Rome, I'm pretty sure he would've hit it . . . many times.

I find it very comforting that the guy who might just be the closest we've ever had to the ideal of a "philosopher king" wasn't some holier-than-thou saint, who just floated through life spouting wisdom as if from a divine fountain.

He struggled, like you and me, to live as a good person.

And coming back to the Facebook comment thread I started this post with, Marcus realized that it was a lot easier to live a good life if you weren't walking around with a chip on your shoulder.

36

Head Games

In the attempt to make meditation more accessible and engaging, a lot of device and app developers have been incorporating ideas from video games, working to "gamify" the experience.

One brainwave-sensing device lets you count the number of bird chirps before you lose focus, and as you "level up" you get to hear different birds.

Another calming device lets you unlock different kinds of musical experiences and vibration patterns by paying more money . . . not unlike those games my 12-year-old plays where for only 5000 more "gems," (which cost $9.99 in the real world), his in-game avatar gets some shiny new powers!

But by far the most common tactic is to keep a running streak of how many consecutive days you've been meditating. (One of my students sheepishly admitted that he'd once fired up the app during a long meeting, not so he could meditate, but just so that he would keep his streak going . . . and I bet he's not the only one.)

So does gamifying meditation work? Absolutely, if the goal is to keep people engaged with the app/service/device.

But is that really the goal? For the developer sure, but hopefully not for the meditator.

During the pandemic there was a glitch in one of the leading meditation apps that resulted in everyone's consecutive-days streaks getting reset to zero. So say you had a 45-day streak going, when you finished that day's meditation the counter showed a paltry "One Consecutive Day!"

People were FURIOUS!

The app's customer support team and social media feeds were swamped with outraged meditators . . . if you can imagine such a thing. The developers had to scramble to correct the record so that people's streaks were restored.

But why was that so important?

After all, the people knew they had a pretty good streak going. What did it matter that the system didn't display exactly how many days? What does it say that the "official tally" of their streak was so important that losing it led people to, well, lose it?

I think this might be the root problem with the gamification of spiritual practices like meditation.

It uses external validation for a practice that, when approached somewhat differently, is meant to free us from leaning so heavily on outside approval. And gamification creates metrics by which the experience can be judged a success or failure. It creates winners and losers. But if you look at meditation, or life for that matter, as something to win or lose at . . . then you've already lost.

Don't get me wrong . . . I'm not totally against meditation apps or devices. I think anything that gets anyone into meditation is a great thing. Apps in particular open a door for a lot of people to begin exploring meditation, but that doesn't mean the path they put you on is one you should travel for long.

There are other doors, and other paths.

Maybe find one that leads to a place where having your consecutive-days streak snapped due to a system error cause you to react, not with a howl of protest, but with an amusing chuckle because you realize how silly it was you ever took it seriously.

An app developer once asked me if I wanted to do a meditation app. I thought told him the only app I'd want to put out would be one that would teach you to meditate . . . and then delete itself after 30 days so that you could no longer rely on it. He thought I was crazy.

37

Afraid of the Dark

Enlightenment has the word "light" baked right into it.

So naturally, people on a spiritual path tend to think of themselves as moving towards the light, and away from the dark, whatever those words might mean for them.

This is why you'll find a lot of practitioners of New Age spirituality who insist that everything needs to be at a "high vibration," or that they need to banish all negative thoughts—the former describing the dullest music ever, the latter being impossible.

Because the vibrational waves of which music is made have both crests and troughs.

Positive implies negative as surely as dark implies light.

Stories need both good and bad characters to be worth telling.

There's no such thing as a Yinless Yang. (But, as my friend Tim Brunelle points out, it would be an awesome band name.)

The Yin-Yang symbol is so overused, plastered onto everything from t-shirts to tankards of ale, that it's become a stock spiritual icon, like the namaste emoji, easy to dismiss.

But pause for a moment and you'll see that the light and dark halves of the namaste symbol are not only equally in balance, but that each contains the seed of the other. Together they make the whole. You can't have one without the other.

Darkness is as much a part of the spiritual life as the light.

Spiritual Bypassing is the term for using spiritual techniques and ideas to suppress, paper over, and generally avoid dealing with some of the darker realities of what it means to be a human being.

Don't do that.

Especially not during tumultuous times, when we tend to get ourselves all stirred up, and might seethe with feelings we would really rather not admit to.

Everyone has a shadow, both literal and metaphoric.

Running away from anything is just another way of hanging onto it.

Awakening, enlightenment, inner peace . . . call it what you will . . . doesn't arise when we finally learn how to "fully embrace the light," or when we raise our vibrations high enough, or cleanse or purify or whatever . . . but when we stop being so afraid of the dark.

Ironically, we can also be afraid of the light too. See #115.

38

Knowledge Ain't Nearly Enough

Everyone is addicted to something to some degree. It could be your phone. Or binge-watching late into the evening. It could be working too much. (They don't say *workaholic* for nothing.) Or it could be the classic addictions, the ones they have 12-step programs for.

One thing I've noticed about addicts is that most KNOW their addiction is hurting them, and often those they love. But that knowledge is filtered through a fog of rationalization, apologies, shame, promises to stop . . . anything that allows them to keep doing what they're doing.

So clearly, just knowing something is bad for you isn't enough. And this applies to everything from heroin to those cookies you keep on the upper shelf to make them harder to reach . . . but not hard enough.

What's needed is a different kind of knowing, a deeper knowing. I like to call it awareness. A moment when you see the truth of your situation with crystalline clarity, unclouded by judgment, shame, or blame.

Here's an example . . .

I used to be addicted to video games. It was one of the things that was ruining my relationship with my wife. I would come home late from work, stressed out, and rather than deal with her and begin the painful process of talking things through I would dive into my Xbox and not come up for hours.

One night I came home at about 10:30. She was already upstairs in bed. Relieved, I went to the family room . . . but something was missing. There was a hole where my Xbox should've been. I walked into the kitchen to get a drink and there on one side of the double-sink, submerged in about 18 inches of the clearest water I've ever seen, was my green-and-black, special Halo Edition Xbox, cords and all.

It was strangely beautiful.

And the first thought that popped into my mind, with that crystalline awareness I spoke of earlier, was, "She's right."

So I made my way upstairs, and tried to climb quietly into bed. My wife, who'd been unable to sleep, who'd been awake for hours, girding herself for battle, rehearsing the argument she was sure we'd have, hissed, "Did you see it?"

"Yes," I replied. "You're right." And then I leaned over and kissed her on the forehead and went to sleep.

I never played video games again.

Sometimes the event that jolts us into the awareness that leads to change is kind of funny, like my drowned Xbox. Sometimes it's horrific.

I was lucky. I only lost my Xbox, not my wife.

I don't tell this story to brag about how I became a better man thanks to my steely reserves of willpower.

As if.

Truth is, I needed something outside myself to shock me into that awareness that led to making a change for good.

I hope you're not held as tightly in the grip of an addiction as I was. But I'm guessing that there's some problematic habit that you really, really, really know needs addressing. But so far just knowing that hasn't been enough.

Maybe this story can cause a little crack to open, so that a sliver of that awareness shines through.

For a deeper dive on addiction and meditation, see #50—Filling the Hole.

Maybe.

39

_____ is Not
Your Meditation

My first foray into meditation was a flop. I tried for about a year, dabbling in different Zen practices, but it didn't work, and I gave up, convinced that my mind, and my life, were too crazy to meditate—then waited 15 years before giving it another, more successful, go.

For the years in between, whenever the conversation turned to meditation, I would say, "Cycling is my meditation," because it felt sucky to admit that I couldn't meditate to people who obviously could, and because it was kind of true . . . or at least I hoped it was.

In the years I've been teaching, I've met enough people to fill a small concert hall who've told me that gardening or running or knitting or cooking, or whatever is "their meditation."

Just the other day I was at my favorite cycling café, sipping coffee and scarfing down a post-ride almond croissant, when one of the guys in the group asked what I did for work, and upon hearing I was a meditation teacher said, "Cycling is my meditation."

I laughed and told him that I know why he said that, because that's *exactly* what I used to say before I learned to meditate.

And then I said, "Look, I don't want to harsh your mellow, and I'm not suggesting that cycling isn't awesome, but it's not meditation."

I said that when people say things like that, they're inserting an invisible equals sign between those two activities.

Cycling = Meditation

But mathematical equations are supposed to be reversible, which means that Meditation = Cycling should be equally true, but it's obviously not.

So why does he, and so many others (and maybe even you), feel that a particular activity is the equivalent of meditation?

I explained that when people say that cycling or gardening or whatever is "their meditation," what they're really saying is that they've found an activity that, more often than not, allows them to escape their brain chatter. (He admitted this was true.)

And because being free from your racing thoughts is such a rare experience for most people, who spend most of their time stuck in the distracted, noisy layer of consciousness Buddhists call "Monkey Mind," they think of it as meditation.

But it's not.

What they're really experiencing is what it's like to be fully present—to be immersed, in the moment, without your mind yammering away.

And it feels wonderful.

I told him that after I learned to meditate—and, more importantly, learned how to make it a daily habit—I soon began to experience the same quality of presence that I used to only experience when riding my bike, when I was engaged in all kinds of mundane, everyday experiences that no one ever thinks of as meditation.

Like waiting in line at the grocery store. Or sitting in a meeting. Or listening to music while stuck in rush-hour traffic. Or hanging out on the playground with my kids. Or whatever.

Wherever I was, and whatever I was doing, I was just in my life, not in my head—which was surprising because I used to be in my head so much that I thought it was normal.

Until I discovered it wasn't.

One of the greatest joys I have as a meditation teacher is when I can help others come to the same happy discovery. That happiness flows not from managing to find more time to spend doing the things we love, but to love more of whatever we might be doing in all the times in between.

40

Do Gooder

Have you ever politely held the door open for someone who waltzed through without even acknowledging the gesture? And have you then thought, or perhaps even said, under your breath, something not so nice about that person?

Yeah, me too.

The hardest thing about that situation isn't shrugging off the other person's rudeness. It's acknowledging that we weren't really doing the good deed for them. We were doing it for us, so that we could play the part of a good person, and we need them to notice so that we can get validated and feel better about ourselves.

So it's really a transaction, masquerading as kindness, in which we give something to get something, and the anger we feel is because the other person isn't holding up their end of the deal.

Because, be honest, if we were really holding the door open as a selfless act of service, why would we care if they thanked us?

If Mark Zuckerberg really cared so much about public health in San Francisco, why does he need his name plastered all over the hospital?

Is a good deed less good if unacknowledged? Or is it better?

In the *Bhagavad Gita*, Krishna drops a tasty bit of wisdom on Arjuna that gets at the root of this question:

To action alone hast thou a right and never at all to its fruits; let not the fruits of action be thy motive.

Meaning that the highest good comes when we act for the sake of action itself, rather than for any kind of personal reward. This is the path of dharma, of duty, and acting in alignment with dharma is the most fulfilling life we can lead.

And while quoting the venerable Gita, and using words like Dharma and Duty, seems to push this into a lofty realm, the principle really does apply to something as small as holding open a door, or something as squishy as picking up dog poop.

None of this is to say that we can't enjoy someone noticing and acknowledging our good deed. (Or that it's somehow wrong to thank people for doing nice things.)

But the "thank you" can't be your reason for doing it.

41

Peace Out

Did you know that September 21 is the International Day of Peace?

I didn't until that morning when I read a very angry Facebook rant from someone promoting the day while at the same time bitterly complaining about . . . well, it doesn't matter what they were complaining about.

But it simply goes to show that Peace with a capital P, while certainly a noble cause, is not actual peace. And peace activism is often taken up by people who can claim very little of it in their own lives.

In the late 1990s I was living in Venice Beach and walked past a king-size white sheet a neighbor had nailed to the wooden fence in front of his bungalow, on which he'd painted, in blood red letters, probably smearing the paint with his clenched fists, the command:

STOP ALL WAR!!!

It was like, "KICK WAR'S ASS!!!"

And all I could think was, "How warlike."

Pretty much everyone in the neighborhood knew that the guy was an angry, bitter and inconsiderate asshole. He certainly wasn't a man of peace. In fact, it would be more accurate to say that he was at war with the world and, as his neighbors, we were the most likely casualties.

I'm not saying all this to dump on those who feel called to promote peace. I'm just saying that it helps to understand that true peace can only come from people who have found it first within themselves.

And while it can be surprisingly easy to connect with that place of abiding peace through meditation, I know from my own experience that it's hard to stay connected, and to consistently act from that place in the service of peace when we open our eyes and step back out into life.

But it sure helps to know where we can go to find it again.

42

It's No Thing

I want you to consider something that at first will seem ridiculous. And after you grasp the idea it may well seem useless.

OK . . . still with me?

There are no things in this world.

No nouns, only verbs.

No objects, only processes.

Consider what we refer to when we use the noun "whirlpool." It's just a pattern of swirling water, energy moving through the medium of water. Same thing with waves. Also walks, and conversations. You can't have a walk without walking. You can't have a conversation without talking. Think of any noun, any noun at all, and you will see that it's simply an enduring pattern of action.

Even a rock—the thingiest thing most people usually think of when I ask them to explore this concept—is just a snapshot in time of a boulder on its way to becoming dust.

This principle holds true even for the thing we are most existentially certain about, that deep down there is an entity called

"I," a definite feeling that, as Descartes famously postulated, "I think, therefore I am."

But what we call a self is really, as both ancient sages and modern neuroscientists will tell you, simply the act of consciousness turning back on itself. It is a process of "self-reflection." In fact, you don't have a self without reflection.

This is not a bad . . . thing.

The best experiences of our lives, when we are in what's called a flow state, are when we totally lose our sense of being a separate self, when we are free of our brain chatter and merge fully into the state of being.

And being is a verb not a noun.

We may have a strong sense of being separate from the world, of being this distinct bit of awareness contained within the boundaries of our bodies. But this is an illusion, a flickering reflection in the mirror of our minds. It's nothing, really.

A couple years after learning to meditate The Beatles released a song, *Across the Universe*, which contained the refrain, "Nothing's gonna change my world."

It wasn't until after I learned to meditate myself that I realized I'd misunderstood that line.

It wasn't that meditation allowed me to become this super-stable person of unflinching equanimity . . . like the statue of the Buddha I kept in my bathroom . . . that would remain unperturbed by the events unfolding around me.

No, what my daily practice of meditation led me to understand was that what The Beatles were talking about was that it was the daily experience of no-thing-ness, of pure consciousness, that was important. Because that was the experience that allowed me to know I was something other than, much bigger than, the little self-centered me that was the source of all my struggles and frustrations.

And that changed my world.

And it will change yours, too.

43

Clarity

Unclouded vision is always better, no matter what it sees.
— the author

Many years ago I taught a couple to meditate. They were having trouble in their marriage, and had heard about how meditation had helped my wife and me through a tough time. Though they didn't say so explicitly, I got the very strong feeling they were hoping that learning would also give them a tool they could use to work through their problems, to heal, and emerge as a stronger couple—another meditation success story.

But that's not what happened.

Although meditation allowed my wife and me the clarity to see that we were meant to work through things and stay together, this couple saw just as clearly that their paths were meant to diverge.

They got divorced about 8 months later, amicably.

Ask them today and they'll tell you they think of it as a success story. Because even though the outcome was the opposite of what they hoped for going in, they were able to make a tough decision without a lot of rancor, or needing to blame each other, because they could both see it was the right one.

Clarity is the key.

Because when we make big life decisions in a fog of stress and uncertainty, we can end up second-guessing and regretting, sometimes for the rest of our lives.

Establishing a daily practice of meditation is always a life-changing proposition. Often those changes are the kind that leave people with a kind of good-vibe glow. They lose weight, start to loosen the grip of addictive behaviors, smile more at the little things in life.

But many of the changes that meditation brings are much more disruptive.

I've taught people who've ended long-term relationships, abandoned what seemed to be thriving careers, given up lifelong habits and moved on from some dear friends.

Change, even uplifting, life-enhancing change, can be damn hard, even when you can see clearly what needs to be done.

But at least you can see.

44

Three Steps Back

I'm sure you've heard the old adage, "Two steps forward, one step back." It acknowledges that the path of progress doesn't always move in a forward direction.

But what happens when you seem to take three, four, or even more steps back . . . with not one that you'd put in the forward basket?

What happens when you fall in a hole?

Depression, severe illness, or those less-dramatic times when you just seem to be stuck, swirling around in some eddy, with a bunch of dead leaves, while the forceful current of life sweeps on by for others?

I think the opportunity is to let go of the embittering idea that things shouldn't be this way, no matter how shitty or unfair they might be.

The opportunity is to accept the truth that you are where you are . . . and here's the hard part . . . to understand that there is nothing you could have done differently.

You may have had options, but you made the choices you made. Other people made theirs. The world unfolded as it did.

Nothing about that is wrong. You are not wrong for being where you are.

That doesn't mean that you can't make different choices going forward.

That doesn't mean there's nothing you can do.

That doesn't mean you can't get unstuck.

But it sure helps if you can let go of regret. If you can stop wasting energy beating yourself up. If you can cut down on all the should-haves and should-nots.

Life, as long as it lasts, always affords us the opportunity for change. It could be tomorrow. Or the next day. Or it could be right after you finish reading this.

Will you take it?

45

Behind the Mask

We learn as kids that it's fun to dress up, to put on a mask, and pretend to be someone or something else.

And it's especially fun at Halloween when strangers give you candy for doing so, even if your parents only let you keep a tiny portion of the loot.

And well into adulthood we love to get all gussied up for a costume party—a tradition that dates back to the grand masked balls of London in the 1700s.

But what if you had to wear a mask forever?

What if you didn't even realize you were wearing a mask?

As it turns out, this question points to a core spiritual truth: that the person we identify as when we get home from the party and take off the mask is actually still a mask. That our sense of being an individual self is an illusion, that life is a kind of grand costume party.

"But," people say, "I'm me . . . I'm a person, I can feel it in my bones . . . I know it."

Me too. But, what is a person? Is it the body? Certainly not. Every cell in your body is replaced every 7 years or so, some lasting longer than others. The body is a flowing pattern of cellular death and regeneration. But you have a sense of self that is older than your cells. So this sense you have of being you is something that transcends the body.

So what then?

The word "person" is taken from the Latin *persona*, as in *dramatis personae,* as in the cast of characters in a play. Back before microphones and amplifiers, actors wore masks with megaphone mouths to project their voices out to the audience. The *-son* in per-son refers to the sound of that projection.

So person = mask.

The person you know yourself to be is, in other words, an act. It's a role you play in this production we call life. The word personality is actually closer to the truth, because we know that a personality is a fluid thing, made up of ideas, behaviors, memories . . . ephemera really.

We live in a society strongly oriented around our personalities, about identifying as and expressing who we are in all the witty, whimsical and photogenic ways social media platforms allow.

And yet everyone, even the most-followed Instagram influencer, has this little seed of doubt, a voice from deep inside, that leads us to wonder, "Am I just this solitary little awareness sewn up in a bag of skin? Is this . . . all there is?"

If our answer to this existential question is "Yes," we usually go down the path of hedonism, distracting ourselves from that doubting voice, trying to pack as much into however many years we have left.

But if the answer is "No," or more often, "I'm not sure," we might get pulled onto the spiritual path, leading us into practices like meditation that allow glimpses, fleeting though they may be, of what we are other than this, glimpses not of the me, but of the we, that we really are.

So what are we, really?

Well, although the saying of it is definitely not it, we are the life-force power of the universe experiencing itself as us, through the mask of our personhood.

We are the universe/god/wholeness . . . it doesn't matter what you call it.

We are each playing our unique role, the one we were assigned at birth, our part in the great play of the cosmos.

As Kurt Vonnegut so playfully put it in his wonderfully whimsical novel, *Cat's Cradle:*

> *Oh, a sleeping drunkard*
> *Up in Central Park,*
> *And a lion-hunter*
> *In the jungle dark*
> *And a Chinese dentist,*
> *And a British queen —*
> *All fit together*
> *In the same machine.*
> *Nice, nice, very nice —*
> *So many different people in the same device.*

And the best part is that beginning to realize this truth doesn't mean you dissolve into some detached, nameless, amorphous cosmic ball of light.

You still get to wear the mask, you still get to stroll around the stage as you, and people will sometimes still give you candy.

One of my favorite bands from high school has a great song based on that bit of whimsy from Vonnegut. Do a YouTube search for "Ambrosia Nice, Nice, Very Nice."

46

Ego Tripping

Maybe you've heard some version of the joke:

So a meditating, macrobiotic, intermittent-fasting vegan walks into a party.
How do you know?
Because they told everyone in the first five minutes.

When I got back from spending 4 months in India, completing the immersion phase of what was an 18-month journey to be a Vedic Meditation teacher, I told EVERYONE, and found a way to work it into EVERY conversation.

I was insufferable.

And that's because there is no ego trip quite as potent as the spiritual ego trip.

But the irony is that while it's the ego that drives us to learn to meditate, to give up our career and change our lives to become a meditation teacher, or to become enlightened, or woke, or self-actualized, or to achieve cosmic consciousness, or whatever, it's also the ego that blocks our progress along the path we've so proudly, and loudly, proclaimed.

Why?

Because everyone, including the highest and most-esteemed yogis, has an ego. (Why do you think some of the biggest scoundrels are those who walk a spiritual path?)

And the ego has no interest in letting go of any power. As it turns out, the ego quite likes ego tripping.

So then, why can spiritual, contemplative paths lead to a less-egocentric us?

Well, it's not because they allow us to achieve anything worth boasting about, even though the ego might, for a while.

No, it's because the spiritual path invites us to step into practices in which the ego, that prickly-proud part of us that wants to achieve something, is revealed for what it truly is: an aspect of us, not the entirety of us.

You have an ego, but you are not your ego.

And in the transcendent oneness of pure awareness that meditation can allow us to experience, the bonds by which the ego tried to hold itself firmly in the center of ourselves begin to loosen.

And loosen.

And . . .

Awakening is not something the ego can achieve by trying or wanting. Or even by trying not to want. Egos don't wake up, as much as they might insist they can.

Awareness wakes up to itself, as you.

And if your ego decides to take the credit, at least for a while, Awareness doesn't mind at all.

47

I Learned a New Word Today

The word is *atelic* (pronounced ay-tee-lic), which means an activity done for its own sake, not to achieve any particular goal or end.

Like goofing around with your kid, blowing bubbles, hanging out with friends, going for a walk, watching the sunset—ordinary, everyday joys. It also applies to things like dancing and singing, and plinking around on a piano . . . unless of course you're a professional at any of those things, in which case the activity becomes more pointed and purposeful, more *telic*.

And I realized that one of the biggest pitfalls of social media is that it's turned so many of what used to be atelic activities—things we did simply because we enjoyed them—into things that can be quantified and judged.

So posting that cute picture of my son and me playing can now be something that gets me x-number of likes, comments and shares. Ditto with the picture of my lunch. And so on.

If those posts don't get as many likes . . . does that mean we enjoy them less?

If we're being honest . . . yeah, maybe a little. Maybe the pic isn't as cute as we thought. Maybe our friends are bored of us posting so many shots of food, maybe . . .

The insidious thing about social media is that status-seeking and validation are baked right into the pie, and so insecurity (or pride) is always peeking its head around the corner.

Now I'm not saying you should give up social media. I'm not. (Although I have dialed it way back.)

And I'm not suggesting you refrain from posting about the little joys of life. I'm not going to do that either. And clearly, it's unfair to ask that you not be affected by how much, or little, what kind of reaction those posts receive.

I think it's just good to be aware of the dynamic at work. Because awareness is the first step towards freedom.

And because playing silly games with your kid is worthwhile, even if you're the only two people who ever know.

48

What's the Rush?

There's a big biohacker who has a program, a very expensive, very exclusive program, that purports to pack the equivalent of four decades of sitting in Zen meditation into five days of intense neurofeedback.

No, really.

I'm not saying the program isn't powerful, or potentially life-changing. And I think neurofeedback is an intriguing tool.

And I know it's possible to undergo a huge change in a flash, whether it's on a psychedelic journey, or a long walk in the mountains, or just sitting in meditation with or without a lot of wires attached to your head. I've experienced such moments of expanded awareness myself, and have witnessed others have similar experiences.

But back to the program in question, the whole 40-years-of-meditation-in-5-days thing. I think it's the hucksterish hubris of the marketing promise that's worth reflecting on, because it seems antithetical to the very essence of what sitting in meditation for 40 years would actually be about.

I mean, after the first 10 years or so (which I'm guessing would be sometime early on the second day of the 5-day program), wouldn't you transcend the part of you that was in such a hurry?

Can you imagine the Buddha coming to his awakening under the Bodhi Tree and then asking himself, "OK, so how could I have done that in a tenth of the time?"

And yet the hype one encounters along the spiritual path is unrelenting.

I know a breathworker who claims that a 90-minute session of hyperventilating to a killer DJ mix is "the equivalent of 10 years of therapy."

The other day I saw a meditation teacher advertise what's essentially an intro webinar to sign up for her meditation course as a "Free Master Class in Stress Management."

I heard of another teacher who told a guy who was on the fence about attending an expensive, 10-day retreat in India, "Well, you should know I've had people reach enlightenment on my retreats (wink, wink), and so you should think about that."

And just earlier today I saw someone was offering an online Chakra Balancing course for $249, but then took pains to explain how when you added everything up it represented "a $2499 value," but that the deal was expiring soon, so click now!

What's going on here?

I think at the root of all this hustle and hype is a deep insecurity that we're not where we should be on the path of life. And so if someone promises we can get there faster, that we can make the leap from beginner to master without having to navigate all those intermediate steps, and maybe save a few bucks . . . where do I click?

Breathe . . .

One of the most liberating gifts we can receive is to not be in a hurry. But it's a gift that only we can give ourselves.

At some point it helps to realize that things take as long as they take. Life is not a race, and the person who reaches enlightenment the fastest doesn't get the biggest trophy.

Which means you're not lagging behind, so you don't have to rush to make up for lost time . . . because there's no such thing as lost, or wasted, time.

Every moment of your life has brought you to this exact point, and it's exactly where you're supposed to be.

You can't storm the gates of Heaven. If you try, you'll get there out of breath, dripping with sweat and they'll just send you back to take a shower.

49

Loosen Your Grip

I love a good Rumi quote as much as the next spiritually oriented person. To think that so much wisdom could have been expressed so beautifully by one person, so many centuries ago . . . mind-boggling.

Here's a quote I used to have on my wall.

> *Life is a balance of holding on and letting go.*
> — Rumi

That's so true.

The only problem is . . . how do you know when to hold on and when to let go? How do you know if you should move on after a painful breakup, or work for hours to assemble the perfect playlist to get back together? To quit your sucky job, or suck it up for another year?

Hey Rumi, how about some practical instructions . . . maybe a Quick Start Guide?

In my experience, the first step toward being able to find the right balance between holding on and letting go is to learn how to loosen our grip, to not hold on so tightly.

There are two situations in which we tend to grip too tightly:

1. When we're starting something new.

2. When we feel we're losing control.

The first is obvious to anyone who's ever learned to play tennis or golf, to chop things with a very sharp knife, or drive in their first heavy rainstorm. We tend to hold on a bit too tightly to the racquet/club/knife/steering wheel.

Luckily, being made aware that we're gripping too tightly is usually enough. Our teacher might say, "Loosen your grip," and we look down, see the whitening of our knuckles, and realize that we had no idea how tightly we were holding on. And just noticing tension brings a slight relaxation. You don't need to be told to relax your flexor tendons. The tennis instructor doesn't have to pry your fingers away from the racquet.

The second situation is the trickier one. Because no one holds on more tightly than the person who fears they're losing control. And this dynamic applies to the big things in life: relationships, career paths, goals . . . stuff like that. And because the stakes are high, our brain tends to focus on the potential negative outcomes—we'll never love again, we'll never get another job, etc.—and so we reflexively clamp down.

But when we put all our energy into hanging on, we blind ourselves to the truth of our current situation, and also wall ourselves off from the flow of possibility, from situations that might well be better than the one we're clinging to. And ironically, we usually do more to hasten the end of whatever we're trying, desperately, to hold onto.

They don't call it a "death grip" for nothing.

So what does loosening our grip mean when we apply the idea in real life?

It means owning stuff, but not being owned by your stuff.

It means setting big, ambitious goals, but seeing them more as directional beacons than as accomplishments that you must absolutely achieve to be happy. You may accomplish your goals, or the pursuit of them may lead you to better ones. Be open to better.

It means understanding that no one "completes you." That depending on another for your happiness is a trap. It means acknowledging that all relationships go through ups and downs, and eventually end.

Ditto with jobs.

Ditto with everything.

This is not to say we should be disengaged or detached. It doesn't mean living dispassionately.

It's just that those who cling too tightly to life are rarely in a position to enjoy it.

I once saw this play out in the cutest way on a playground. See #76—Letting Go.

50

Filling the Hole

I've been asked to give a talk on addiction.

It's something I know a bit about. My dad was an alcoholic for the first two-thirds of his life. And over the first few decades of my adulthood I've moved through little addictive squalls—video games, sex, dark chocolate—never becoming what you might call "clinically" addicted, but it was pretty clear that I had traits of what Craig Nakken, in his excellent book, calls *The Addictive Personality*.

I read that book after I'd been meditating for a year or so.

And what I learned is that addicts are desperately trying to fill a hole. But the sad truth is that no matter how much booze, sex, drugs, or shopping they pour in . . . the hole is still there. No matter how many fans or followers you get, no matter how many companies you start, no matter how many houses or cars you have, it will never be enough.

The only remedy is to realize that there is no hole.

Only then can you stop frantically trying to fill it.

Only then can you feel a sense of wholeness.

(I love the etymological irony that *hole* and *whole* are so similar, and yet so completely different.)

Sounds good. But how?

In my dad's AA meetings people spoke of a higher power. Something bigger than themselves that could help them get beyond the insatiable neediness of their individual egos. AA doesn't work for every alcoholic, but it worked for him.

Meditation is what worked for me. Because it allowed me to have a direct experience of that layer of consciousness, the experience of pure being, in which I am whole.

It wasn't an instant fix. It didn't mean I didn't have a lot of work to do . . . that I still don't have work to do. But it was a great foundation from which to start.

There's a reason the 11th step in all 12-step programs is meditation.

My dad, who I was privileged to teach to meditate a few years before he passed said, "It should be the third step!"

I think he might be right about that.

51

Nurture Nature

With two outgoing, social kids we meet a lot of parents. And a lot of prospective parents seem to be drawn into our orbit as well. A while back we were at a playground talking with a woman who was obviously, uncomfortably pregnant. But she was excited, you could tell, her brain stuffed full of baby books and eyes glimmering with anticipation.

"I can't wait to see how the whole Nature vs. Nurture thing plays out," she said.

(pause)

My wife spoke first. "No, no. There is no versus. Children have a nature and a parent's job is to detect and nurture it."

The woman raised her eyebrow. This wasn't the answer she'd expected. "It's only when you make it a versus thing do you have real problems," I added, probably needlessly, because I always have to say something.

Those of us with kids know. There's a person there, a unique personality, at 4 or 5 months. I'd say that person is there even earlier, but we lack the tools to detect it, and babies can't do much more than burble, eat and poop to express themselves.

And this essential you, the you who you have always been, lies beneath all of the surface layers of identity that we typically lean on to define ourselves—like your job description, your political affiliation, your sense of style, your likes and dislikes, below even your most deeply held beliefs. And certainly below the level of your problems.

In fact, it's fair to say that many of the most-vexing problems we struggle with arise because we become disconnected from our essential selves.

We don't, truly, know our nature.

And if we don't know that, how can we nurture it? Perhaps our parents never really understood us (perhaps because they didn't really understand themselves), and pushed us into molds that didn't fit. It's not their fault. They were doing the best they could.

The good news is that as meditators we have a wonderful tool with which to reconnect to our core selves, to ground ourselves in who we really, truly are and always have been. The Veda teaches that this essential self is happy, whole and complete. It wants nothing. It needs nothing added to it. It is the source of all the happiness and love we've ever felt.

That is our nature. And meditation is how we nurture it.

52

Enthusiasm

Mythologist Joseph Campbell's much-repeated credo "follow your bliss" sounds good, but can be hard to put into practice.

Especially when we stumble across the message in the middle of a busy life, filled with obligations, many of them decidedly bereft of bliss.

So we think, "Yeah, that would be nice . . . but not for me, and certainly not today."

I get that.

But I think we might be better able to heed, and benefit from, Campbell's instruction if we didn't interpret it to mean that we have to throw some big lever that abruptly switches our whole life onto a more-blissful track.

I think a more actionable plan would be to have a look at your life and see how much time you currently spend a week on things that are pretty much the opposite of following your bliss.

More like follow your dreck.

Follow your constant irritation.

Follow your mind-numbing, binge-watching habits of distraction . . . the things you do pretty much just because they're the things you do, not because you enjoy them.

And see if you can carve out just an hour of that time to do something you can do with enthusiasm.

The word "enthusiasm" comes from the Greek *enthousiasmos*, which roughly translates to "in God," or "having God within."

Because it's when we are enthusiastically engaged with life, when we are doing something in which we are fully present, usually with a smile on our face, that we are following our bliss, that we are on the path of truly living our life.

Here's an example to show you just how small a thing this can be:

My wife LOVES swing dancing. I am a terrible swing dancer, so she's done very little of it in the 20+ years we've been married. Yesterday I was teaching a workshop and so she decided to drag our 11-year-old along to Golden Gate Park, where they offer free swing-dancing lessons.

On the way home from my workshop, I rode my bike through the park and stopped when I saw a big crowd of people happily bopping along to the beat of a swing band. There must've been about 100 dancers and so it took a while to find her in the twirling crowd.

But when I did?

Her smile was radiant, her step lively, she was the embodiment of bliss, she was beautiful.

I sat there watching her for a while and then rode on, smiling.

I hope she does it again next week.

53

The Right Side of Wrong

If I asked, would you rather be right or wrong?

Duh. You don't even have to think about it.

We *love* being right.

And the struggle over who gets to claim that title has been the source of countless religious wars, extreme political polarization, and continuing conflict with the people we love most as we argue over who's right in even the most mundane aspects of life.

> *In every partnership, there is a person who loads the dishwasher like a Scandinavian architect, and one person who loads the dishwasher like a raccoon on meth.*
> — @ColeyTangerina, a funny person I found on the internet

But . . . would you rather be right *all* the time? Or are there times you'd rather be wrong? Maybe even big-time wrong?

Being right all the time means there is nothing left for you to learn.

It means you already know everything.

It means you're incapable of growth.

How boring. And insufferable.

Nobody likes a know-it-all.

(P.S. I'm the Scandinavian architect in my family.)

54

Reboot

Almost everything will work again if you unplug it for a few minutes, including you.
— Anne Lamott

When I teach a meditation course, people are often surprised that I strongly suggest they carve out 10 to 20 minutes in the middle of even the *busiest* afternoons to meditate. Not before bed. Not when they get home, but right in the middle of the busiest part of the day.

But, but, but . . .

I have so much to do.

People will think I'm a slacker.

It feels weird to meditate at work.

I'll probably just think about work stuff, so what's the point?

Good question.

The answer begins with acknowledging a couple of important truths:

1. We all get to a point where the demands of the day begin to wear us out. Way too many meetings, too much data to process, too many things on our To-Do list, so many competing agendas. We get fried, foggy-brained, flustered. You know the joke about Eskimos having way more words than we do for snow? Well, I bet the number of words we have to describe this all-too-familiar state of burnout is probably higher.

2. And when we experience that state, whatever word we use to describe it, our performance suffers, often dramatically. We make more mistakes, we tend to be quicker to anger, and patience goes out the window. And I'm not just talking about work performance. In every major city in America, there are more fatal car crashes on the commute home than the commute to work. Because no one is at their best when they're fried.

So un-fry yourself.

A short meditation break is the best, easiest, cheapest and most-accessible way I know for us to unplug, to close all the useless browser windows in our brain, and enjoy a nice, re-energizing and stress-relieving reboot.

Who says, "I'm at my most creative and most collaborative at 5pm?"

People who choose to meditate at 3pm, instead of jolting themselves past the mid-afternoon slump with a shot of caffeine or sugary snack.

So do yourself a favor.

Do your sleep a favor.

Do your waistline a favor.

Do your coworkers a favor.

Do your friends, family, pets . . . heck, do everyone you might come into contact with a favor.

When the day is spinning out of control, and you have way too much on your plate, and you're getting a bit frazzled, don't just do something . . . sit there.

Like a Tree, Not a Pillow

More and more I have come to admire resilience.
Not the simple resistance of a pillow, whose foam
returns over and over to the same shape, but the sinuous
tenacity of a tree: finding the light newly blocked on one side,
it turns in another. A blind intelligence, true.
But out of such persistence arose turtles, rivers,
mitochondria, figs—all this resinous, unretractable earth.
— Jane Hirshfield, *Optimism*

I recently gave a talk at a big high-tech company on the topic of meditation and resilience.

Because resilience in the face of change and adversity is a much-desired quality in companies these days, be they high-tech or low.

And meditation has been demonstrated in studies and by countless anecdotal accounts to increase our capacity for resilience.

Afterwards, a woman came to say that what I'd said reminded her of a poem by Jane Hirshfield.

When I got home I Googled it, loved it.

And I realized that my talk at the tech company had been mostly about the pillow kind of resilience.

Which is not a bad quality, to be sure, especially in my memory-foam pillow.

But companies are not pillows. And neither are we.

And so I think we might learn more about resilience from looking, really looking, at trees.

My absolute favorite photos of trees are by Myoung Ho Lee. Do yourself a favor and google his name + "tree series".

56

Lucky Me

Today I was able to help out in an emergency situation that, had I not been there, probably would've gone way worse. A beat-up old Nissan was stalled in the right lane on a curvy section of Park Presidio, a 6-lane divided section of inner-city highway running through Golden Gate Park. The speed limit is 35 MPH, but people frequently zoom through at 55 or higher.

There was a break in the traffic, so I pulled alongside and noticed that the driver, who looked to be in his late 70s, had a befuddled expression as he kept trying to crank the engine into starting. I figured we had about a minute before the light behind us changed and cars would come racing around the corner.

So I pulled over in front of the stalled car, jumped out, and was able to coax the driver to get out of his car and stand on the side of the road. I went back to turn on the emergency flashers just in time to see another car coming up fast in the right lane, oblivious to the situation, and I jumped out of the way as it plowed into the back of the Nissan.

The crumple zones crumpled, the airbags deployed, and the collision was so forceful that it shoved the first car several feet forward into—unfortunately—the back of my car.

Damn.

The driver of the second car, a shiny new Honda, was another old guy, who seemed to be in shock, so I helped him get out of the car and turned on his emergency flashers, hoping to prevent yet another collision.

Insurance information was exchanged, tow trucks hauled the wrecked cars away, a nephew showed up to take the Honda driver home, and I ended up driving the owner of the Nissan home because he didn't have a phone and couldn't call anyone.

I was telling the story later to a group of friends, and one of them said, "Lucky you were there."

I know he meant that it was lucky for the other driver, the one I pulled out of the car before it was rear-ended, and that's true.

But tonight, as I was sitting down to write, I thought . . . it was kind of lucky for me too.

I mean, it was terribly inconvenient, causing me about a 90-minute delay, and now I have to take my car into the body shop, and the accident will go on the CARFAX report, and my resale value will go down and . . .

What a hassle.

So why do I feel so OK about it?

I think it's because being there put me in a position where I could help another human being, even if it was a stranger I'll likely never see again.

I was able to be useful in a way that really mattered. It made my day in a way I'll never forget.

Luckily, life is constantly putting us in situations, most of them thankfully not so dire, in which we can be of service, to do something that matters for someone else.

Deep down, isn't that what we all really want?

57

Better Than a Car Crash

Yesterday I wrote about a car crash I witnessed and got to help with.

And today insurance adjusters are looking at photos, measuring skid marks, and going over the facts of what happened just before the crash so they can assign blame.

But for me the most interesting thing isn't what happens before, but after a crash.

Statistically, getting into a car accident is one of the most common precipitating events that lead to big changes in our personal lives. I'm talking about job changes. Cross-country moves. Breakups. Marriages. A decision to have kids.

And it doesn't even have to be a major accident like the one I witnessed. Even a fender-bender will do. There's something about the *impact* that jolts us out of a state of complacency.

We look up and realize . . . it's time to make a change.

Sometimes the impact is metaphoric.

The event that puts an addict into rehab and onto the path of recovery is often some horrible, humiliating experience—described as "hitting bottom"—in which the ego surrenders, a newfound clarity emerges, and addict says to themselves, "I can't live like this anymore."

Happily, learning to meditate is another event that often leads to big, positive changes.

Because, in a much less dramatic way, meditation can free us from the grip of the ego and provide the clarity and perspective we need to see what we truly want, first by showing us what we no longer want.

See #67—
The Opposite of
Going Gonzo.

I call it the "meditation effect," which is better than "spiritual whiplash."

And you don't even have to file an insurance claim.

58

Pay Attention

It's a great phrase, because attention is currency. In fact, it's the universal currency. And no one has more attention to pay than anyone else.

And it's what we choose to pay our attention to that determines what we truly value, and determines the quality of all our relationships.

If you're not spending time together, sharing experiences, your relationship suffers.

Which is why parents who buy everything for their kids, but don't spend time doing things with them, don't end up having very good relationships with their kids.

If you don't spend quality time exercising. your relationship with your body is degraded.

If you are constantly distracted, with multiple browser windows open, always checking your phone, multi-taking your way through life, your relationship with the present moment suffers.

Because that's how relationships work.

Here's a very ordinary example of what I'm talking about:

I have two young boys, so my daily parenting includes a constant struggle over screen time.

The other day I was trying to nudge my oldest son off his iPad so he could walk the dog, something he's generally pretty good about.

But not that day.

"Aw . . . can't you do it Dad?"

After a bit of back-and-forth, me cajoling, him whining (teenagers are champion whiners), I said, "I could . . . but ask yourself: would you rather have a good relationship with your dog, or a good relationship with your iPad?"

He switched off the iPad and took the dog for a walk.

This made the dog, the dad, and the kid very happy.

(Full disclosure . . . it's not always that easy to pry him away from his device.)

59

Dis-Ease

It's easy to feel at ease when things are easy.

This is the appeal of upscale, all-inclusive vacations where you are catered to and fussed over like some posh purse dog.

But can you feel at ease when things are going to hell?

Can you be at ease even when disease is knocking hard at your door?

These are the questions that have recently bullied their way to the front of my brain. Because my wife—my lovely, loving and wonderful wife—is dealing with a life-threatening lung condition . . . and the only treatment option is a transplant.

Fuck.

I'm not telling you this to get sympathy, although I'm pretty sure a wave of love, well wishes and care emojis will be rolling in soon. (And from the bottom of my heart . . . thank you.)

This is the first of series of essays that deal with my wife's medical situation. See also #64, #68, #75, #78, #81 and #82.

I'm telling you because not telling you is becoming awkward. Like I'm hiding something that I, that we, don't want to hide anymore.

We've started telling people. Started talking with the kids. Started telling our kids' schools. Started telling friends. My wife, normally a VERY private person, recently posted about it for the first time on Facebook, which was a huge step for her.

And since I mostly teach from my own experience, I wanted to tell you.

Because this, like all experiences, certainly has something to teach. And as our path unfolds through whatever this ends up being, I'm sure there will be lessons I want to share with you.

But I can't do that if you don't know.

So now you know.

Here are the questions that I'm asking myself these days:

Can I be at ease when things aren't easy? (And what does that even mean?)

Can I accept what I really, really want to reject?

Can I see what's right when so many things are wrong?

I don't have the answers. But sitting with the questions helps.

And meditation helps.

And telling you helps, even though I'm not sure why.

60

On Beauty

I recently stumbled across a very intriguing definition of beauty:

Beauty is the experience of something which one does not wish to change.
— Anonymous

Meaning we see/taste/hear/feel something and no part of us thinks, "You know what would make this better?"

We appreciate it as it is, in the moment, for what it is.

No change necessary.

Except . . . change is constant. So we watch the gorgeous sunset and know that the sun will set and the colors will fade.

The beauty of music is that the notes dissolve into air.

We see a flower in full bloom and know that its petals will soon fall away.

In fact, I think that the certainty of change is a big part of *why* we find something beautiful.

There's a tension that adds juice to the experience.

And this is why fake flowers are so disappointing. I mean, who among us hasn't seen flowers from a distance and then, as we got closer, discovered they were plastic? The letdown you feel, at the moment the fraud is detected, is the sudden release of that tension.

The things in life we find beautiful are only beautiful because they won't last. This is also true of life itself.

Many years ago, long before I ever took my first step along a spiritual path, I went to the funeral of an old girlfriend, one of the great loves of my life, who died in a car accident. Her parents were Buddhists and on the altar at the back of the room there was a little card with this phrase written in a halting hand:

> *Everything that has a beginning*
> *Has an ending.*
> *Find beauty in that.*
> *Make peace with that.*

It can be hard sometimes to find that beauty, to make that peace.

And it can be even harder to resist the desire to cling, to keep things just as they are, just the way we like them.

But it's worth a try.

For a philosophical and poetic take on the nature of beauty see #82—A Beautiful Distortion.

61

The Discomforts of Travel

I am writing this in Istanbul, land of my mother, on a long, COVID-delayed vacation to visit relatives in Turkey, to show my boys a very different part of the world.

And absorbing the experience through my sons' eyes, ears and taste buds (one of them is totally open to trying new foods, the other not so much . . . thank God for the universality of french fries and pizza) has reminded me that yes, travel broadens the mind, but only to the degree that we're willing to tolerate the discomfort of being in situations that are first disorienting, and often unpleasant.

I think this principle also applies to inner travel.

When people start meditating they are usually surprised when first confronted with the sheer volume and the utter randomness of 95% of the thoughts that arise in the mind.

It's like being a stranger in their own mind.

And when the thoughts are unpleasant, often about things they'd really rather not think about?

Well, in those situations you can see why a guided meditation would be appealing.

Guided meditations allow us to replace (for a while) our caustic inner voice with someone else's nicer, calmer voice. Instead of listening to our own mind yammer away about all the things that we and other people in the world are doing wrong, we get to listen to someone talking about compassion, or gratitude, or just inviting us to imagine a series of pleasant things: like waves lapping at a tropical shore, or a blanket of warm, glowing light emanating from our heart chakra, or . . .

But what happens when that nice voice stops talking, stops offering instruction, and the harsh inner critic comes roaring back? What happens when the meditation music stops and we're left with the uncolored, unfiltered content of our minds?

Well, at that point we have a couple of choices:

We can fire up the app and find another guide. And with the plethora of options (one app claims over 140,000 guided meditations on tap), with an almost absurd degree of tactical specificity—Big Breakup Meditation, My Uber Is Late Meditation, and so on—so we can keep distracting ourselves from our inner voice pretty much forever.

It's like putting up a poster to cover an unsightly crack or stain. It doesn't do anything to fix the problem, but at least we don't have to look at it.

Or . . . we can patch the crack in our relationship with our own minds.

We can sit in silence and simply allow our thoughts to flow. We learn that we're not here to fight the experience, not trying to have fewer or nicer thoughts, not here to control the mind. We learn to see that the part of us that judges some thoughts as good and others as bad is just more thinking. We learn to be a neutral observer, not even judging ourselves when we discover that we're judging ourselves.

We see that the part of us that wants to shelter in the comfort of someone else's voice is kind of like my kid defaulting to the salty, fried, familiar comfort of french fries. It's understandable, but it's not really the path along which we grow.

Growth comes from learning to be your own guide, to effortlessly navigate the stream of consciousness without trying to control or direct it.

Meditation can be a wonderfully conscious-expanding practice of inner travel in which you come to feel at home within your own mind.

But only if you allow it to be.

62

Heavenly

Just watch children playing.
Eat vegetable soup instead of duck stew.
— Matsui Basho, *Advice to Poets*

I don't like the idea of people stressing out, fighting their way through San Francisco traffic, rushing to be on time for meditation.

Seems a little counter-productive.

So I usually start my public meditation sessions with 15 minutes of what I affectionately call chit-chat, where I take random questions about pretty much anything, meditation-related or not. The questions range from the esoteric to the nitty-gritty practical.

The other night a couple came in, sat on one of the couches along the wall. The guy raised his hand.

"Do you teach Astral Projection?"

I said I did not.

They left.

They were seeking after an experience, something very specific, something fantastical, and I wasn't going to be able to give it to them.

Good to know what you want.

There's a lot of experience-seeking on the spiritual path. People seeking relief from the dreary tyranny of the ordinary. And there are certainly experiences to be had. You can chase them for a l-o-n-g time.

But the real spiritual journey is the one that brings you full-circle back to where you started, to the mundane, the everyday, the ordinary.

Except that it's not anymore.

Not because it's different, but because you are.

Because if bliss, freedom, enlightenment or whatever you call it exists, it has to be found now. And not just in some kind of special now, but in every now.

> The kingdom of heaven is spread out upon the earth but men do
> not see it.
> — Jesus, *the Gospel of Thomas*

What does that mean? It means that heaven is not some special place you go when you die if your spiritual GPA is high enough to grant admission.

It means that it's here.

Now.

It's in the sound of the TV in the next room, in a dog begging for treats, in a child's exasperated sigh, in a couple making love, in a kid popping a wheelie, in that funny, flatulent sound of an almost-empty ketchup bottle, in the swirl of rainwater tumbling into a storm drain, in the crack of the ball off a bat, in the wispy whimsy of clouds . . . the list is, thankfully, endless.

Heaven is the *most ordinary* place.

63

The One You're With

I grew up during the ebb tide of the hippie days. My dad was an officer in the Air Force, and a staunch Republican, so he was a kind of buffer against that tide, but a lot of things seeped through.

And there's a Crosby, Stills & Nash song from that time, a kind of flower-power anthem, that said if the person you loved wasn't around . . . well, that you should just *Love the One You're With*.

Back then the song was about freedom, about not being limited by physical constraints like proximity, or by the conventions of polite society and promises of fidelity, about LOVE written in big, flowing hippie letters.

Like people have ever needed encouragement to cheat.

Tonight I was going down a streaming-music rabbit hole and happened upon that song, which I hadn't heard in years.

But something about it struck me differently. I realized that loving the one you're with doesn't have to mean sleeping with the groupie on the bus, or the administrative assistant, or your yoga teacher.

Loving the one you're with could also mean loving yourself, as you are, right now, warts and all.

It could mean rejecting decades of social conditioning that happiness is contingent upon getting things in your life to work out the way you want, that you won't be happy *until* you achieve this, or buy that, or get promoted, or get whomever you currently fancy into bed.

It could mean rejecting the idea that you're this flawed person who will only be truly lovable after successfully completing this 5-step program of self-actualization.

Now that doesn't mean I expect you'll feel a swelling in your heart chakra when you peek at your bank balance, or your belly hanging over your waistband, or whatever it is you might be trying to change.

That's a feeling. I'm talking about taking a position.

I'm talking about the kind of love that accepts things as they are, that is fully present, that doesn't waste energy or attention on shame or blame.

Loving the you that you are now doesn't mean giving up. Or being passive. It means having your feet firmly and fully planted in the present moment, because it's only from that more-grounded state that we can take whatever might be the next best step forward along the path of our evolution.

As Krishna says to Arjuna in *The Bhagavad Gita*, explaining why meditation might be helpful to a busy, stressed-out warrior like himself, "Grounded in being, then perform action."

Or as I like to say to people who find themselves beating themselves up for making too many mistakes as they rush around trying to get everything done, "Don't just do something, sit there."

64

Happy Thanksliving

Since opening up about my wife's medical condition, it's been surprisingly hard for me to be on the receiving end of all the love and well wishes. It's as if the container I've built to hold everything together has started to crack. There's the impulse to hold firm, to keep it all together, but at the same time a growing understanding that the container has to collapse, that I have to let go if I am to be truly present and thankful for our life as it is right now.

And it being Thanksgiving, a holiday my wife LOVES, I found myself going way back, thinking about how it all started, to what life was like for the people in the beginning, before it was a holiday.

So what if you stripped Thanksgiving of all its pageantry, its football games, its pumpkin-spiced merchandising, and of all the salivating over those Black-Friday and Cyber-Monday deals waiting to be gobbled up?

You'd find a group of cold, hungry, frightened people coming together to express gratitude for the simple fact that they were still alive. Against all odds, in a harsh new land, with winter fast-approaching, and no certainty for what was to come . . . they were alive.

And they knew, and were thankful for, that the food they were feasting on, and their continued survival, depended heavily on the kindness, expertise and generosity of strangers.

As I write this, my wife, and our family, and all who love her/us are facing a very uncertain winter. And we depend heavily on the kindness, expertise and generosity of strangers.

The fact that there is even a procedure called a lung transplant is a miracle. It's good to remember that.

And it's also good to remember that life itself is a miracle.

There's an interesting book, *A Fortunate Universe*, by the astrophysicist Geraint F. Lewis, which details the incredible array of circumstances that had to be just right for life as we know it to even be possible.

Guru Deva, the last great master of the Vedic tradition out of which I teach, said, "It is a great gift to be born into a human body. Even a single breath is precious."

If we can remember that, and give thanks, not just for the overflowing bounty of the harvest, but for life itself, for however long it lasts, we have a much better chance of honoring that gift.

65

Spoiler Alert

All perfectly known futures are the past.
— Alan Watts

I often hear people say they wish they knew what was going to happen.

But would you, really?

It would be like someone telling you the end of a movie.

You would hate it.

We all love cliffhangers.

Hanging at the edge of unknowing.

There's a tension there that makes you feel . . . alive.

Life is tension. We are rubber bands stretched between birth and our eventual death.

Stretching into the unknown is how we grow.

We might start out on a spiritual path seeking answers to life's fundamental questions, often because we reject the ones we've been handed by our parents, our religion, or our peers.

But then a funny thing happens.

We learn that the real value of answers is that they lead to better questions.

We learn that the biggest questions have no answers.

And over time, bit by bit, in ways we never could have predicted, we may find that we can even be comfortable in that uncertainty.

66

Plowing the Field

5,000 years ago, no one described meditation as defragging your hard drive.

No guru ever said that to be fully present is your default font, or that the reason you're so distracted is because you have too many browser windows open in your brain.

But these are the kind of metaphors I use all the time to describe what meditation is and how it works to improve our minds, our bodies and our lives.

Many years ago, just after I started teaching, I was in South Carolina, talking to a couple of my older cousins, both of whom have spent their lives farming. They had heard from my mom that I was teaching meditation, and they wanted to know what this "Hindu stuff" was all about.

I quickly found the phrases that worked so well in San Francisco kind of left them scratching their heads. I don't mean to suggest it's because they are ignorant yokels . . . they're some of the smartest people I know. But all the tech talk to explain why anyone would pay to learn to sit there with their eyes closed doing "nothing" just wasn't clicking with them.

So I explained that the brain is like a field. It gets dried out. The mind gets crusty and worn into ruts. And I explained that meditation, and the release of stress it brings, is like plowing that field. It breaks up the ruts, opens up the soil, so that seeds can sprout, take root and grow. No farmer would ever waste good seed on an unplowed field. On this we could agree.

But this isn't just a farm-friendly metaphor. Science shows that regular meditation changes our brains. It plows, so to speak, the neural hardscape, all those repeated patterns of thinking and stress and worry that degrade our lives and undermine our happiness.

The impulse to improve our lives is a deep and sincere one. Every New Year's Day, people all over the world wake up—some with hangovers—and resolve to do all kinds of things (some, surely, resolve to stop drinking) in the hopes of becoming a better version of themselves.

That's really what resolutions are—the seeds of the better life we hope for ourselves. We know it's possible . . . but a month later, most of us have already given up.

Why? Is it because our resolutions weren't sincere? Is it because we're weak and lack willpower?

I think it might be that when we cast the seeds of our intention onto the hard-packed soil of our brains, with ruts worn deep from stress . . . well, is it any wonder so few of them really take root?

This is why I talk of meditation being a foundational habit, a way to make the field of our minds a more fertile place. It's like upgrading our firmware, so that we can run all that Good-Person 3.0 software—to return once again to the familiar phrasing of our times.

My cousins aren't ready to meditate yet. But I think the crusty topsoil of their skepticism may have softened a little.

67

The Opposite of Going Gonzo

Dip into any self-help media stream and you will be flooded with ads, articles and videos from influencers pitching programs for extreme weight loss, extreme fitness, extreme debt relief, extreme makeovers of every kind.

We are told that to make real change happen we have to go "all in."

And for many years, a very large man has made millions of dollars by stomping around on a stage flanked by banks of towering loudspeakers, literally screaming at people about the necessity of taking "MASSIVE ACTION!"

Now, I'm not saying that some people haven't been helped by following this advice. But one of the downsides of having these examples and ideas thrust on us so often, and so loudly, is that it makes real, substantive change seem intense, scary and hard.

And so when we think about making some positive shift in our life, the task can seem overwhelming, because we think it has to be all or nothing. And faced with that daunting choice, it's all too easy to do nothing. To turn away, to put off starting, to have another beer, or doughnut, and poke around a bit more on the internet. To lapse back into the habits of inaction and distraction that keep us stuck in the ruts of life.

But real, life-altering change doesn't have to be hard. Or dramatic. Or scary. Overcoming the inertia of our habits and actually changing the course of our lives can be a pretty easy thing to accomplish.

OK . . . but how?

The same way one of those giant ocean-going tanker ships manages to change course. A fully loaded container ship can weigh up to 300,000 tons (that's the equivalent of 100,000 elephants), and has a massive amount of inertia, and a GIANT rudder.

The force required to turn that huge rudder would be enormous. So the helmsman doesn't turn the rudder. Because a long time ago nautical engineers realized that if they put a tiny rudder on the trailing edge of the big rudder—something called a trim tab— they could use it to turn the ship. They make a small adjustment to the trim tab, which requires only a small amount of energy to move, and as it turns, the pressure of the water flowing past the tab ends up turning the big rudder, which then turns the ship, easily.

In other words, minimal action leading to massive change.

A daily practice of meditation is like that trim tab. It's a relatively easy thing to do. You don't have to change into special clothes, you don't have to go anywhere, and there's no sweating or stomping or screaming required.

When we meditate we break up the ruts in our thinking. We dislodge some of the stress from our body. Those are the things that keep us stuck in the reactive, habitual patterns we'd like to change.

And freed from the negative habits of mind and the shackles of stress, we find it a little easier to make those small daily choices that, little by little, end up making big shifts in life not just desirable, but doable.

68

Stumbling Toward Enlightenment

So I'm sitting here, late on Xmas Eve, listening to my wife's ragged breathing, with her oxygen concentrator droning away in the next room, and wondering what kind of topical, holiday-themed message I want to share with you given what's currently going on in my life.

So I took a peek back at what I wrote at this time last year.

Um . . .

Let's say it's a pretty blunt example of putting something out there, attempting to sound wise about it, and then having life hand you that exact situation, in a way you could never imagine, to see if you can walk the talk.

You can go back and read that post, #20—*Gift Wrapping*, but I'll paste the most salient bits here:

> *It means that, instead of throwing up our hands in despair when something "bad" happens, we challenge ourselves to do the work to find the opportunity, the "good," embedded in it.*

We can ask ourselves, "What do I have to do so that, years from now when I look back at the current horrible, effed-up situation, I can say, 'That was one of the best things that happened to me.'"

*It's not easy, but it **is** a skill you can cultivate. (end excerpt)*

So then . . . how am I doing cultivating that particular skill?

Well, I have to admit that I'm a long way from ever being able to say that my wife suffering from a degenerative lung disease that's left her housebound, on 24-hour oxygen support while we wait for a transplant is "one of the best things that happened to me."

A very, very long way.

In fact I kind of want to punch myself for writing that.

But I can say that I've been able to appreciate the hell out of all the incredibly sweet, loving and beautiful moments that have punctuated the suffering and sadness.

I can say that I've discovered a gentle patience that has surprised me . . . .and my wife.

I can say that my sons and I have never been closer.

And I can honestly say there hasn't been a moment during this whole process where I've complained that the situation is wrong, unfair, or wailed that she's too young, that it "shouldn't be happening."

Because it is most definitely happening.

So this is me, on Xmas Eve, with a dying wife lying next to me, waiting for a lung transplant that might save her life, having to face up to something I wrote in what I didn't know were much, much happier times.

Stumbling toward enlightenment.

Aren't we all?

We struggle, like that guy who was supposedly born on this day, under the weight of our particular crosses.

I may be a bit further along the path than you . . . or not. One can never really know, and should certainly refrain from making any bold claims.

But life will definitely show you where you are, if you have the courage to look.

69

Sarcastically Yours

The root of sarcasm is the Greek verb *sarkezein*, which originally meant "to tear flesh like a dog." From that developed the noun *sarkasmos*, "a sneering, hurtful remark."

Yikes.

So sarcasm is speech that's meant to cut. To make a joke at someone else's expense. The tearing of flesh.

It's also lying, because when we're being sarcastic we usually mean the opposite of what we say.

"Wow . . . smooth move," we sneer when someone accidentally makes a huge mess.

"Nice jacket," we say to the underdressed friend at the dinner party.

I could go on, but you know what I'm talking about.

And if we wield the sharp sword of sarcasm too often, we end up hurting ourselves, because people assume we're being sarcastic those few times when we're really being sincere.

Part of becoming a better person means taking on new practices and habits. But it also involves giving up things that no longer serve us.

It was very hard for me to give up sarcasm. That groove had been well-worn by my years as a smart-alecky advertising guy. But over time I let it go and made two happy discoveries:

1. All my important relationships improved. Turns out being a smart ass isn't that endearing.

2. You can be just as funny by being sincere.

And I say that without a hint of sarcasm.

70

Kick the Bucket List

Lately I've been thinking and writing a lot about facing the reality that our time on Earth and our capacity to get things done is finite.

You will never, ever, ever get everything done.

You will never find yourself "on top of things."

So rather than frantically rushing around, trying to get it all done—employing endless optimization strategies, downloading productivity apps, and buying expensive day/week/month planners—you might try taking your foot off the gas, consciously doing less, and enjoying whatever it is you choose to do with the time you have.

And while this makes a lot of sense, some have said they find this line of thinking a wee bit depressing, as it reminds them of the certainty of death.

Exactly.

You, and I, and everyone will die. This is the great inescapable truth, but because it's uncomfortable, people get themselves twisted into all kinds of knots trying to escape it.

But there is great power, and quite a bit of relief, in keeping the thought of death close at hand. The Stoics called this idea *memento mori,* and would contemplate death daily, even going so far as to carry a little reminder in their tunic pocket.

Because it's only the certainty of death that makes any of our actions meaningful. After all, if you were immortal, it wouldn't matter how you spent your time, because your supply would be never-ending.

It you like poking around on Etsy you'll find a wide collection of memento mori talismans, coins and other ways to keep this reminder close.

This is why near-death experiences are so transformative. You come face-to-face with the truth that you are going to die, and that every moment matters, including this one.

But this is not, as one person asked, a reason to jam as many peak experiences into whatever time we have left by creating what's called a "bucket list."

I think the bucket list is just another scam cooked up by our achievement-obsessed society, and it helps perpetuate the false idea that it's chasing after these big, peak experiences that make life worth living.

(It's also worth pointing out that quite a number of people die when trying check something of their bucket list. Oh, the irony.)

Happiness, a sense of purpose and meaning, a feeling of peace with what is . . . these don't come from chasing peak experiences, nor from getting everything we want. They come from flowing with the present, from wanting what we get, and not resisting life as it flows across the transom of our experience.

Running from the reality of death doesn't work. And you won't live a better life if you chase after it.

Luckily, you don't have to.

Happy New Now!

Yesterday was a truly glorious New Year's Day in San Francisco, and that's not often the case.

The soaking rains broke for the day (they'll be back tomorrow), the sun came out and so did thousands of smiling, strolling, hiking, biking people all cheerily wishing each other, "Happy New Year!"

I dare say people were noticeably nicer to each other in traffic.

And everywhere you could feel the brimming hopefulness of all those freshly minted resolutions, the palpable sense that life could be, would be, better.

How long does that last? When do you stop saying Happy New Year? 10 days . . . maybe 2 weeks?

What happens when the effervescent fizziness of all those resolutions starts to go flat? What happens when the year is no longer so new? Is it just back to the same old grind?

Or . . .

Maybe you step back and realize that there's actually nothing at all special about New Year's Day.

Yes, I know that the collective enthusiasm that bubbles up on the first of January does have a tangible short-lived effect . . . but really, it's just a day. No different from any and every other day.

This is not the buzzkill you think it is.

Because it opens to an understanding and full appreciation of NOW.

Because now is always new. Now is the very essence of new.

The never-ending, indivisible present moment is always brimming with potential.

The thing worth celebrating is that every day can be a kind of New Year's Day.

Every day is a chance to wish someone happiness. To be nice in traffic. To resolve to be better. To learn something new. To chip away at a bad habit, or begin to build a new one.

You can do that every day.

You can do that now.

72

Buddha Baby

Have you ever looked into the big, wide, unblinking eyes of a baby?

It can be a little unsettling.

They take in everything. But they don't think about anything.

Babies come into the world fully aware, but people who study infant cognitive development believe that they don't think, in the way you and I do incessantly, until they're about 14 months old.

Think about that.

This is why babies experience no separation between themselves and the world. They don't have a sense of being a separate self. They experience the unity of oneness that ancient sages and modern quantum physicists tell us is the underlying truth of the universe. They are all little Buddhas . . . but they don't know it.

And then come what parents call the terrible twos and threes, what cognitive development scientists call the stage of individuation, where babies start to run into the uncomfortable truth that there are other people in the world, and sometimes those other people want different things than they do, and so . . . tantrum!

It's a messy, noisy, but necessary stage. Because as frightening and painful as discovering the experience of separation can be, it's the basis of empathy, sharing, and love. After all, you can't share your firetruck with the other kid in the sandbox unless you first think of it as yours to share.

You can't fall in love with someone else until you recognize that other people exist.

So as babies we all came into the world grounded in the experience of a great truth . . . and then we lost it. And that hurts.

But as we bump along as these solitary little selves, we get to have experiences and cultivate practices that allow us to rediscover the fundamental truth that everything is one.

This is what falling in love is really about . . . discovering the intimacy of unity in the form of another.

This is why we can become easily awed in nature, or by looking up into the vastness of the sky and feeling so small, and yet still a part of it all.

And this is why we meditate.

To experience what we are beyond our thoughts and feelings, to be grounded in something deeper than our To-Do list. To have the experience of being fully present, fully aware, like a baby . . . but with the ability to know it, and in that knowing, to treasure it.

We can learn a lot from babies.

73

A Beautiful Mess

Sometimes during my meditation workshops I tell a story about my most anal-retentive, control-freak friend, Dan. (Dan isn't his real name, but when he found out that I tell this story, he asked me to use a fake name.)

Dan resists the term control freak. He prefers to think of himself as a "control enthusiast," simultaneously softening and reinforcing how controlling he is.

Anyway, one day I took my friend "Dan" on a hike through the woods near our house. After a few minutes, I noticed that he seemed a bit ill at ease, like something was bothering him.

Turns out, it was the forest that was bothering him.

"It's so . . . messy," he said, gesturing weakly toward a clump of trees off to the right.

I was, rare for me, speechless.

It had never occurred to me that anyone could have that response to nature.

But, seen from his perspective, he was right. There were broken branches scattered everywhere from the night's windstorm, dead leaves and rotting logs cluttering the ground. At one point, we passed the half-eaten carcass of a large bird, maybe a blue heron, and he asked how long I thought it would be before a ranger came and cleaned it up.

The forest is a messy place.

When people learn to meditate, they frequently have a similar reaction.

They come complaining that their minds are tangled places, full of anxious thoughts and uncomfortable feelings. They think I'll serve as a kind of park ranger and teach them how to sweep the paths clean so that their thinking is more orderly, more focused, and that I'll help them clear away the dead, stinky things that pop up now and then.

But the flow approach to meditation I teach is about allowing everything to be as it is, not concentrating or focusing, not trying to have fewer or nicer thoughts. I teach them to be OK with their messy minds.

Because here's the thing . . .

The beauty of the forest comes not in spite of, but because of how untamed and untidy it is.

I think the mind is the same.

Yes, it can be messy.

And meditation can help reduce the stress that is the source of our most agitated and anxious thoughts. But the idea that life would be better if more of our thinking was more organized and structured misses the fact that the most beautiful, creative and insightful thoughts you ever have had, have risen up, unbidden, on their own, totally at random.

This is why nobody in all of history has ever filled in the blank of the phrase "I think of my best ideas _____" with "when I'm trying to think of them."

Neither I, nor you, nor anyone has any idea what their next thought will be. And that's wonderful.

Life is the same. It's unpredictable, and never seems to work out the way we planned, no matter how much we obsess over those plans. Life isn't just full of twists and turns, it's the twists and turns that make life interesting.

You can try to tidy up the forest, or discipline the mind, or control life, with mixed results.

Or you can lean in the other direction and learn to appreciate the raucous, messy beauty of it all.

74

Center of the Universe

Did anyone ever accuse you of thinking you were "the center of the universe?"

Well, you are. In an infinite field every point is the center of the field.

So congratulations, you *are* the center of the universe! But before you get all puffed up . . . so is everyone else. So is everything else. No point is more central than any other. Ancient Vedic wisdom, and modern quantum mechanics, tell us that we live in a self-referral universe. That reality is actually a relationship between an observer and the observed.

There is no such thing as a singular "objective reality." You are simply a point from which the universe observes itself. So the question is, what do you choose to see?

I'm not sure if you've seen the thought-provoking documentary, *The Social Dilemma,* but it digs into the fact that we are hard-wired to be more triggered, more engaged by content that stirs up our deepest fears and insecurities.

Which means that, from a neurological perspective, you actually catch a lot more flies with shit than honey.

Which means that, especially in these tumultuous times, we have to make a conscious choice about what we want to see in the world.

Not to ignore all the crazy stuff going on, but instead to stop ignoring everything else.

Luckily this is incredibly easy to do. You can close your eyes and bring to mind something you feel grateful for. You can get up and go for a walk, putting your phone on airplane mode . . . or better still, leaving it at home.

Or you can simply tilt your eyes up from wherever you're currently reading this sentence and find something beautiful upon which to rest your gaze.

It could be the enormity of the sky.

Or the light shimmering off leaves.

Your beloved pet napping in the sun.

It could be anything.

Your choice.

What kind of universe do you want to be the center of?

75

Breath Taking

I stood at the end of the hospital bed, squeezing my wife's feet as the nurse pulled the 18-inch breathing tube up and out of her trachea. It made a wet, rasping sound as it was removed, and was immediately followed by a wincing, painful cough that bent her body forward and clenched her eyes shut.

But then, after months of being on 24/7 oxygen support, after a grueling 10-hour, double-lung, transplant operation, after being on a ventilator in the ICU for a week, she sat up, her eyes fluttered open, and she breathed in on her own.

It was . . . breathtaking. That really is the only word.

We have an expression we use to describe situations in which we feel an overwhelming sense of awe.

We say, "It took my breath away." But I don't think that's right.

I think what we actually do in those moments is breathe *in.* Maybe in delight, or surprise, or in wonder, but the breath comes rushing in.

We might hold it a little longer than usual, and so maybe the exhale, when it comes, is a bit more pronounced, and so with the feeling of awe ebbing we notice that our breath is leaving, is being taken away.

Hence the expression.

But in those moments the breath is not being taken from us. It's being given. It's the sudden, involuntary inrush of air, of prana, of the life-force power of the universe that is the sign we've been allowed to witness something miraculous.

Like being able to breathe with a new set of lungs.

Or watching your wife take that first, unassisted breath of fresh air.

The very first thing a newborn baby does is breathe in.

The last thing we do as we die is breathe out.

> *It is a great gift to be born into a human body. Even a single breath is precious.*
> — Swami Brahmananda Saraswati

I think he's right about that.

76

Letting Go

Sometimes the things we hold onto hold us back.

And so we are told, again and again, to "Just let go."

And it seems so easy . . . but we don't. We cling to relationships and jobs, to beliefs and habits, even though we know they no longer serve us.

Why?

Last weekend I was at a playground in Golden Gate Park where I saw this little girl, perched on the play structure about 2 feet above the sand. She was holding onto a pole and you could see she wanted to jump so badly. Her mom was encouraging her to jump. But she was afraid. She would start to let go, and then something deep inside would cause her to clutch the pole with all her strength.

And I thought, we're all like that.

We desperately want to grow, to have new experiences, to evolve.

But that usually involves letting go of security, of certainty, of the solidity of the known.

And so there's this very palpable, visceral tension that grips us.

Sometimes we can get stuck at that point for a long time. Decades even.

Finally, after much encouragement, the little girl jumped. And of course she loved it. And then her mom couldn't get her to stop.

What's a leap you've never allowed yourself to make?

What can you let go of?

77

The Blue

I was in a session with someone the other day, talking about how lately she's noticed that really valuable insights and ideas come up during, and often just after, a meditation session. She was very excited about a particular insight that had come to her she said, "out of the blue."

We talked for quite a while about her insight and about how it might shift some relationships at work, helping untangle some knots of petty office politics.

This is how these conversations usually go. We get excited by some idea that has come to us, whether it's in meditation, or the shower, or just walking along. And we get so caught up talking about the thing that has come like a bolt out of the blue that we ignore the opportunity to examine what is, in fact, more valuable than any idea.

We ignore the blue.

What is it, exactly?

Well, it's nothing, exactly. Or, to be more precise (and more vague at the same time), it's no thing.

But it's the source of all things, all ideas, all concepts, all insights, all creativity, and innovation. It is the field of potentiality itself. Even the concept of "the field of potentiality" arises out of the blue.

And as I said, it's more valuable than any of those things, in the same way that the goose that lays golden eggs is more valuable than any of the eggs because it's the source from which they emerge.

Meditation has so many practical, measurable benefits—from reduced risk of heart attack and disease, to better sleep, lower blood pressure and so on. And every week it seems there's a new scientific study filled with charts and graphs and numbers that prove meditation "works."

But while that's great, the truth is that meditation worked thousands of years before science could prove it.

Because what meditation really does, what it's done ever since people started meditating, is something that can't be measured, and doesn't need to be validated, by our reductionist, materialist science.

It allows us to turn away from the busy surface of the cluttered and calculating mind and slip into an experience of pure being, of that nameless, formless, is-ness from which all names and forms arise.

It allows us to slip into the blue.

And that's not just worth something—it's everything.

78

Hopeful-less-ness

As you may remember from middle school science, nature abhors a vacuum. But since so few of us spend much time in labs or in space, a more practical way of applying that principle here on Earth is to say that people abhor uncertainty.

We have lots of questions, and absolutely *hate* not knowing. So we rush to fill the empty space with answers, even if we don't have information.

This explains the age-old appeal of paranormal prognosticators, whether it's the Magic 8 Ball, or the psychic at your local strip mall, or the ancient Oracle at Delphi.

Filling in the gaps of uncertainty can be fun, especially when the questions aren't so serious. But it's when we come up against life's biggest questions, that the discomfort of not knowing grates on us.

In those situations, some people are brimming with hope, including the hope that they will be resilient enough to bounce back if they end up being wrong.

Others tend towards the pessimistic, telling themselves things probably won't work out. They would rather lower expectations than be disappointed when things turn out badly.

The important thing to realize is that both optimists and pessimists are telling themselves a story to fill the vacuum of uncertainty and make life a little more bearable. This happens so automatically that it's hard to see we're doing it.

Over the last several months our family's life has revolved around some very big questions.

Back in October, the question was whether or not my wife, who was dealing with a degenerative lung disease, would get added to the transplant list at UCSF.

That question was answered in the affirmative in late December, thanks to a feeding tube that allowed her to gain the weight needed to pass a critical threshold of vitality.

But then came the next question: How long will it be until we get "the call?" And the darker question, lurking behind that one: Will she die before a donor is found?

And the uncomfortable truth was, we didn't know.

People rushed in with answers, telling themselves and us a story that they hoped would be true.

It will all work out.
She will get through this.
God has a plan for you.
It's going to be OK.

But of course, they didn't, couldn't, know.

Yvette was less hopeful, or more honest, depending on how you look at it. She told herself that because of her genetic profile it would probably be several months before a suitable donor was found. This was her story.

I admitted it might be months, or I said, "It could be in the next five minutes."

As it turned out, we got the call that a pair of lungs that might be a good match less than three weeks after being added to the list. But that doesn't mean she was wrong and I was right. It's just what happened.

And now, a few weeks after a successful transplant operation, we're asking another question, one we'll be dealing with for as long as Yvette lives.

"Will her body reject the donor lungs?" Or, put another way, "How will life unfold from here?"

But no one, not even her doctors, who are some of the best lung-transplant experts on the planet, know for sure.

The truth is that life *is* uncertainty. That's what makes it alive with possibility.

The question is, can we sit comfortably in that vibrant uncertainty?

Can we see that both hopefulness and hopelessness are just different kinds of crutches? Can we embrace what I'm calling a kind of hopeful-less-ness that tilts neither one way nor the other?

Can we see that life as it unfolds is richer, more alive, than any story we could ever tell about it?

These are the questions I'm asking on this stormy Monday morning.

And the only answer I can honestly give is, I don't know.

79

Emotional Integrity

Integrity means being all of a piece.

Not divided against oneself.

This is usually taken to mean that one's words and actions are in alignment, and it's certainly nice when that happens.

But I want to talk about a deeper kind of integrity—emotional integrity—about not waging war within ourselves, fighting the big feelings that come with being human.

Lately I've been working with a few people who are struggling with anxiety, fear, sadness, rage . . . awash in feelings they really don't want to feel.

Because the Cult of Relentless Positivity that often passes for spirituality or pop psychology would have you think that it's wrong to have those feelings. That you've got to turn that frown upside down, or tune your crystals to raise your vibration, or stand in front of a mirror and chant "I am happy! I am joy! I am bliss!" But papering over your insecurities with happy talk doesn't really work. Plus, you feel like an idiot shouting at yourself.

Straining to hold a posture of constant positivity is just another form of avoidance. You don't need to do that.

Because there are no wrong feelings. You're not a bad person because you feel bad.

In fact, quite the opposite is true.

Psychologists talk about the importance of emotional diversity. Of how a person who experiences a wide range of both positive and negative feelings, and fully embraces those feelings, is far more resilient, far more mentally healthy than someone who, when confronted with something negative, immediately sticks their head in the spiritual sand trying to find the blessing hidden in the muck.

So don't fight or hide from your feelings. Fighting and hiding are just twisted ways of holding on. And don't try to distract or dull yourself. Pretty much everything society has served up to help us "deal with" our uncomfortable feelings just ends up creating more discomfort down the road. That bill always comes due.

I get that you might not feel so "spiritual" when you're struggling with depression, rage, grief or anxiety. But, and I've probably said this before, we are not human beings put on Earth to have occasional spiritual experiences. We are spirit, here to have the full experience of what it's like to be a human being.

And being human is really, really hard sometimes.

If there's one thing to take away from this it's that you can be a whole person, a person of integrity, even when it feels like you're breaking apart.

80

Silence

Musicians have a deeper understanding and appreciation of silence than non-musicians.

Because they know that silence is the source of notes. More importantly, they understand that even the loudest note can't "shatter the silence," that the silence is still there, even when notes are playing.

The way I try to explain this to non-musicians is to point out that if you play a note on the piano or pluck a string on the guitar, you don't then have to play a note of silence to bring the silence back. Because it never went anywhere.

So what does this have to do with meditation?

In the flow approach to meditation I teach—in which we're taught to think our mantra effortlessly and allow everything to unfold as it does—it's usually quite easy for people to experience a state of blissful inner silence, even in the first session or two. It can last for a moment, or a minute, or even longer.

"That was amazing!" people say. "I wasn't thinking anything . . . and I wasn't even trying!"

The lesson is a profound one: that it's easier to experience that blissful inner silence when you're not trying to silence your mind. You can have deeper experiences when you're not trying to go deep. Because the part of you that would try, and the part that would evaluate and criticize the effort, well . . . those are the noisiest, shallowest parts of you.

But then thoughts return, and it seems like the silence goes away, and so people think they're doing something wrong. They want to know what they can do to bring the silence back, forgetting that they didn't have to do anything to experience it.

The problem is that they see silence and thoughts as an either/or proposition. The many musicians I've taught don't seem to have this problem, or they solve it sooner.

Because they understand that silence is the source of sound, they have an easier time grasping the concept that the silent state of pure being is the source of thinking. That silence is always present, even when the mind is filled with thoughts.

It's not either/or.

Learning this allows us to move away from the frustrating idea that meditation is about silencing the mind (not even the Dalai Lama can do it!), and towards the discovery that you are not your thoughts. You are the pure, silent and ever-present state of being from which you can simply witness thoughts. You don't have to silence your mind to meditate.

This is a very happy discovery.

81

Minding the Store

There's a retail space near me that, over just the last 10 years or so, has been several things: a Chinese restaurant, a burger joint, an art cafe, a pop-up "brand experience store," and most recently a boba place. (Who could have ever imagined that tapioca balls in milky tea would be the confection of choice for kids these days?)

I'm guessing there's a place like that where you live, too.

All of these places, with their different names, signage, owners and unique offerings . . . all occupying the same physical space. We tend to identify with the first category—what kind of place/shop/restaurant—to the extent that when a place is vacant we think of it as nothing, as empty.

But what about the space itself? Is it really nothing . . . until a new occupant makes something out of it?

Let's think about it another way.

I want you to scroll through the photo reel of your life: There you are as a baby, then in elementary school, maybe in youth sports, your first teenage job, your first "serious" relationship, your first home of your own, and so on. We think of those as different versions of us, different job descriptions, different likes and dislikes, different beliefs and attitudes, and lord knows different fashions.

But take a good look into the eyes of any of those photos and I think you'll agree that there's something you recognize as a feeling of what it is to be you, a feeling that hasn't changed, that doesn't change, that is the same today as it was when you were young.

Everything about your life can be different, except that feeling.

This is why old people frequently say "I don't feel any different inside," even as their bodies get stiffer and sorer.

Because we are not the body.

We are not our beliefs, ideas, or attitudes.

We are definitely not our thoughts.

We are not our job title, or our relationship status, or our musical playlists, or any of those other things that we think describe and define the us.

Those are all just aspects of what we might collectively call our personality, or maybe our personhood—and they're pretty similar to the current tenants of the retail space I mentioned at the beginning of this post.

They are the catchy name on the sign, the way the display windows are dressed, the menu of services and goods on offer . . . they are what the space is *at this moment in time.*

And all those things change.

What doesn't change is the feeling, the sense of being you, which is the experience of being itself.

That feeling is like the space, the raw space that retains its potential to be anything, even when it's a Boba shop, even when it's empty, even when the building is razed and some completely new building, or perhaps a small section of urban park, bursting with life, is born from the field of possibility.

I don't know what's happening in your life right now. I don't know who's minding the store at present. In my life everything is kind of falling apart. My wife is back in the hospital as she continues to deal with the complications of her double lung transplant. My kids are struggling, each in their own ways, with the uncertainty and worry. My teaching business is in poor shape, as it's hard to do much when you're juggling all of the above. Oh, and our dog has decided that this would be a good time to start dying of kidney disease, or lymphoma, or whatever it is that's causing his blood calcium levels to spike :(

It can be hard to not get totally caught up in our present circumstances, whether they be dire, or wonderful.

But if we can, at the same time, realize that we are so much more than our present circumstances, if we can identify even a little as that field of pure potentiality, if we can simply allow ourselves to be—well, there's a comfort and stability there that might just be the only thing you truly can lean on, insubstantial though it may seem.

It's certainly not nothing.

82

Autopilot OFF

Most of us live our lives to some degree on autopilot.

This sounds bad, but it's really not. Being able to navigate through the world without having to think too much about what you want to eat, or how the toilet works, or how to get where you're going, allows us to entertain higher-level thoughts, have more interesting conversations, and solve bigger problems.

One of the most discombobulating things about travel is that it requires us to switch off the autopilot and go full manual.

Because we find ourselves immersed in a world in which almost all our familiar patterns are broken.

Everything has to be thought about. Nothing can be taken for granted.

But despite the discomfort that arises, breaking our familiar patterns allows us to realize that the way we're used to doing things is just that . . . a way of doing things. It's not etched in stone. It's not universal. This can be a shock, which can lead to a reflexive feeling of defensive superiority, thinking "our way" must be better. (It's not.)

But once we get over the initial shock of everything being different, if we're willing to pay attention, a new stage opens up in which we can detect the similarity that lies beneath the surface of difference.

And the more we allow ourselves to embrace that experience of unity the closer and more connected we feel to people and places that at first seemed SO different.

Meditation is another way of allowing us to settle beneath the choppy surface of the mind, to transcend thoughts and words and concepts, to go deeper than all our surface-level identities—job description, marital status, sexual orientation, political affiliation, likes, dislikes . . . all the particulars of our individuality—to lose ourselves in the flow of pure consciousness.

Dipping into that shared experience of universal awareness, day after day, allows us to better navigate the world of difference, whether we're at home amidst all our familiar patterns, or halfway around the world wondering, "Um . . . how do I work the toilet?"

83

Flow is not Frictionless

One of the most destructive ideas advanced by the modern Spiritual-Industrial Complex is that somehow we should be able to live a life of nothing but easy-peasy, lemon-squeezy goodness, that we can get everything we want, and all our thoughts and vibrations will be blissful.

This is absolutely not true, not possible . . . and it's not even desirable.

Having everything work out exactly the way you want it to, never having to face any kind of disappointment, never being knocked down . . . That would be a kind of hell when you think about it.

Now I'll admit that compared to being stuck, compared to a life in which we feel like we're just grinding along (and getting ground down in the process), experiences of greater flow can seem deliciously free and fluid.

But they're not frictionless.

Our actions always require some degree of effort, and encounter some degree of resistance.

When an athlete is in the zone, she's facing competition.

If a team (be it athletic or work-related) is experiencing the flow of seamless collaboration, it's usually when the stakes are high and there are deadlines and limits they're up against.

Think of a flowing river. Where is there the most friction? On the edges and at the bottom right? Because that's where the river is GROWING.

Wherever there is growth we'll find friction.

84

Trust Fail

My 12-year-old son was watching a little video called *Trust Fall Fails*. And he was laughing, because he's at the age where it's funny to watch bad things happen to other people.

"I would NEVER do that," he insisted.

I hope that's not true. I hope he learns to trust, to allow himself to be vulnerable.

I know you can't trust everyone, and mistakes are both inevitable and painful. But the bigger fail is to go through life with your hackles up, always suspicious, trusting no one.

I know people like that, and I'm guessing you might too. People who live tight little lives, constricted in fear and mistrust. Bitter, cynical people who know the world is out to get them and refuse to let it.

But in refusing to be hurt, they hurt themselves more than the world ever could.

> *The best way to find out if you can trust someone is to trust them.*
> — Ernest Hemingway

"But, but . . . " the ego starts to flail, grasping for the thick branch of certainty.

How can I be sure?
What if I'm wrong?
What if I get taken advantage of?
What if I get hurt?

Wisdom replies:

You can't be.
You might be.
Ditto.
You'll have the opportunity to grow.

This also applies to trusting yourself.

85

Does it Really Matter?

One day Alice came to a fork in the road and saw a Cheshire Cat in a tree.
"Which road do I take?" she asked.
"Where do you want to go?" was his reply.
"I don't know," Alice answered.
Then," said the cat, "it doesn't matter."
— Lewis Carroll, *Alice's Adventures in Wonderland*

There are two ways to interpret this lovely little parable:

The most common is to reinforce the critical importance of knowing where you're going, so that you know which road to take, so that you don't get distracted, so that you reach your destination more quickly, so that you can then plot the correct path to the next destination. This makes sense if you see life as a long stretch of interlinked goals, and success as a measure of how many of them you accomplish, and how quickly.

The other interpretation, which I present as a counterpoint to the prevailing wisdom, is to realize that not knowing where you're going can actually be very liberating. Which is good, because there are plenty of life situations in which it's totally reasonable to not know where you want to go, or "what you want to do with your life." (As the parent of a high-school senior, these questions are coming up a lot.) And in those situations, what really matters isn't which path you begin to explore, it's that you don't freeze up, paralyzed with doubt, worrying you'll make a mistake.

This paralysis can be a minor annoyance, like when you're in a new restaurant, confronted with a multi-page menu, with a waiter you know is teetering on the edge of impatience, and if you don't order something, quickly, they'll excuse themselves with a terse smile, saying, "I'll give you another minute," and then not return for at least 10.

Or it can be major, like when we're on the cusp of some big life decision and so much seems to hang in the balance.

Curiously, the way out of the swamp of indecision is the same in both situations. It's to realize that the cat was right . . . it doesn't matter that much which option you choose.

Obviously it really doesn't matter if you pick the wrong menu item . . . the worst thing that could happen is you have a less-than-satisfactory meal, and who hasn't sat through a couple hundred of those? But when facing those bigger decisions, when the stakes seem so much higher, when you can feel your body and brain starting to tighten up . . .

Breathe.

Question the belief that you're supposed to know what you want, or how things will work out. How could you?

Let go of the idea that your life could be made or unmade by a single decision—like what school you attend or what job you take.

If you examine the life of anyone interesting you'll see that their lives are full of unexpected twists and turns, of mistakes and course corrections. In fact, it's the twists and turns that make life interesting.

This is not to say you shouldn't care about the choices you make, or choose at random. But clearly there's a difference between not caring and caring so much that you clench up and can't move.

But if we can breathe and relax just a little, we can open ourselves more fully to the present. If we're more present, we can better detect the faint stirrings of charm . . . one of those options seems to tug at us in a way the others don't. We can take a small step along the path of charm without the fear of pitching ourselves headlong into catastrophe. And then we can take another step, and then another, keeping our heads up for what might be on the horizon, perhaps another path that branches off in some delightfully unexpected direction.

And if we're lucky, like Alice, our life can be a grand adventure.

86

Software vs. Hardware

Go to any bookstore and you'll find shelves full of self-help books. Because we find ourselves beset by lots of problems, and because the urge to solve those problems—so that we can be happier, healthier and whole—is a strong one.

But the truth is we don't need another book to tell to let go of anger, eat better, not send angry emails, not stay in abusive relationships, not sweat the small stuff, do what makes us happy, be a better mom/dad/boss . . . and so on.

Those are instruction sets, like software programs, and they are simple enough to understand. What can be more difficult to understand is, why do we have such a hard time running that software? Why do we do the things we know we shouldn't, and not do the things we should?

I think it's a hardware issue. I think it's stress.

Stress makes us frazzled and worn out. It ruins our sleep and literally makes us crave foods that are bad for us. Stress agitates our nervous system, changes the way we breathe, the way our brain works, and makes our heart work harder. Stress pollutes our bodies and minds with a bitter mix of hormones and chemicals, so that we have a hard time doing the things we know we should be doing.

Stress also makes it more likely that we stay stuck in those reactive neurophysiological patterns (otherwise known as bad habits), that end up with us doing things we have to apologize for and often feel bad about.

And while this might be the least-spiritual way to think about meditation, I think of it as a hardware upgrade.

Meditation literally rewires our brains in ways that enable us to be calmer and happier. But meditation affects much more than the brain, because the mind and body are not separate. Meditation allows us to relax. To rest. To recharge our batteries so that we have the adaptation energy we need to deal with the demands of life. Meditation boosts our immune system, lowers our blood pressure and . . . you get the picture.

Once we clean up our hardware we find it MUCH easier to run all that GoodPerson 2.0 software, to bring more of our best self to more of our life.

So the question isn't whether meditation is good for you. It's how good can you be about making it a habit?

Just to reinforce this software analogy a bit . . . it's worth noting that the leading mindfulness conference in the Silicon Valley area is called Wisdom 2.0

87

You Are Here

I love traveling, have always loved traveling, because it's an experience in which our senses become heightened, we become more alive, more attuned to our surroundings.

Part of this is surely rooted in the survival instinct. When a small band of prehistoric humans came upon a new watering hole, it made sense to pay extra-sharp attention, to be on the lookout for possible new dangers.

But being fully present is also the path to a richer, more rewarding life, no matter where in the world we might be.

I have traveled extensively in Concord.
— Henry David Thoreau

That doesn't seem like a very interesting quote, hardly worth quoting at all . . . until you realize Thoreau was *from* Concord, not traveling *to* Concord.

And the point I think he was rather cryptically making is that it's possible to greatly expand your travel horizons without straying too far from home. That travel is more about how we pay attention than how much we pay to head off to some exotic destination.

As a meditation teacher, one of the things I go on and on about is the idea that the quality of your attention is a big factor in determining the quality of your life.

"Be fully present at the corner grocery store" probably isn't on anyone's bucket list.

But maybe it should be.

88

A Beautiful Distortion

This morning I was taking my wife to get her blood drawn at the local lab, a weekly appointment in our post-lung-transplant life. And I was using a squeegee to remove the condensation that had formed overnight on her window. The light was hitting it just right and it was beautiful to see her face, refracted through all those tiny drops of moisture, like a pointillist painting. As I squeegeed down in even strokes the distortion was wiped away and I could see her more clearly, another beautiful sight to be sure, but a bit less *artsy*.

And I was suddenly transported back 25 years or so, back to when I got LASIK eye surgery. Before the operation the nurse told me that one of the things I needed to be aware of is that after surgery I would see halos around bright lights, especially at night. I was told to be very careful. The instruction was repeated a few times, so that I actually got a little worried.

And sure enough, the first time I stepped out at night I could see these big, bright halos around every light, just as she had warned. The halos were the result of distortion, caused by the ring of cells that had been ruptured when the surgeon sliced through the surface of my eyeballs to create flaps that could be folded back while he reshaped my corneas to help me see better. The nurse had told me that as the cells knit themselves back together the halos would gradually fade away, leaving me with crystal-clear vision.

But what she didn't tell me was how utterly beautiful they would be.

"I'm going to miss these halos," I thought.

One of the core Vedic teachings is that our sense of being a separate self is an illusion, a distortion of the truth of oneness. And the idea is that through spiritual practices like meditation we can pierce the veil of that illusion and come into a clearer understanding.

And when it's framed this way, there's a tendency, especially when seen from a dualist perspective, to think of the distortion of illusion as bad, or even ugly, and the clarity of awakening as good—which is a denigration of the human and a veneration of the divine.

This is understandable, but unfortunate.

Because while modern neuroscience and ancient wisdom traditions agree that our palpable sense of being a separate individual "I" is an illusion, the source of all our suffering and problems . . . it's also the source of beauty.

Beauty, as they say, is "in the eye of the beholder." It is not in the world. It is something that we can only perceive through the lens of our individuality.

When you are walking down a city street . . . and come suddenly upon a rosebush blooming against a brick wall, you may be struck and awakened by the appearance of beauty. But the rose is not beautiful. You think the rose is beautiful and so you may also think, with sadness, that it will die. But the rose is not beauty. What beauty is is your ability to apprehend it. The ability to apprehend beauty is the human spirit and it is what all such moments are about, which is why such moments occur in places and at times that may strike

another as unlikely or inconceivable, and it does not seem far-fetched
to say that the larger the human spirit, the more it will apprehend
beauty in increasingly unlikely and inconceivable situations . . .
—Mary Ruefle, *Madness, Rack & Honey: Collected Lectures*

As it turns out, seeing through the illusion of our separateness
really allows us to see how beautiful life is. And I mean that we see
all of it as beautiful . . . the pain, the suffering, the loss, this entire
human experience . . . not just the pretty parts.

89

As If

Remember to always treat yourself as if you are someone you deeply care about.
— Adyashanti

The part of this line that really hits me is "as if." Because it gets to the root of a very deep truth: we rarely treat ourselves with the care and compassion that we show to others.

So it can help to pretend.

To act as if we care deeply about ourselves, even when confronted by our deepest fears and inadequacies . . . you know, those things that invariably pop up when we embark on any path of growth, especially when we begin to wander off course, slipping back into old habits and patterns.

When little kids learn to walk, they wander and weave all over the place, and are likely to lurch off the sidewalk at any moment. This keeps parents on high alert, always scanning for possible danger.

In raising our boys, I've learned there are two ways you can prevent a wayward toddler from toddling into harm's way.

You can snatch their arm or the collar of their jacket and jerk them back, which scares them, usually because you're scared yourself.

Or you can reach out, with a cupped hand, touch their shoulder or head, and gently guide them back into line.

The former is sometimes necessary, especially in a busy city, but the latter is definitely preferable.

This principle also applies when we're the ones guiding ourselves along whatever spiritual path we may have wandered away from.

All true compassion is rooted in self-compassion.

Treat yourself as if you're someone you care deeply about, and soon enough you really will.

90

Closing the Gap

I'm a little embarrassed to admit this, but I don't know when my dad died.

It was years ago, but I couldn't tell you what year without looking it up, and certainly not the date. I know it was hot at the funeral, sweltering in the South Carolina heat, so maybe the middle of summer . . . or early fall?

The truth is, I never had much of a relationship with my dad, certainly not when judged against the idea of what that relationship could've or should've been. He did his best, as they say, but that wasn't very good.

That gap between our expectations and our reality is what I want to write about today, on Father's Day here in the U.S., but I think the dynamic applies in all sorts of situations, and on all kinds of holidays, whenever you're "supposed to be" having a certain experience.

New moms often face this gap when they don't feel the swooning love for their babies that everyone told them they'd feel, and a big sea of postpartum depression rushes in to fill that void.

Valentine's Day is another gap day, when all of society seems to be conspiring to remind you of how lonely you are, or how your relationship is floundering, that you and your sweetie might not be as happy together as all the other happy-acting couples jammed into the restaurant with you.

And every spring there are a lot of high-school seniors and families posting proudly on social media about the great colleges they got accepted to for the fall . . . and a ton of other kids and families who are forcing a smile, saying congratulations, but feeling deep down like they don't measure up.

I could go on, but I'm pretty sure you know what kind of gap I'm talking about, right?

For me, Father's Day has always been a big gap day. And I would usually deal with it by not dealing with it—by staying off social media so I don't have to see all my friends posting about how great their dads were, and how much they miss them. I would usually tell my wife and kids that I want to spend much of the day alone, maybe go on a long bike ride, and ask them not to make a big fuss about it.

But this Sunday I got up early, sat in that gap, sniffly and sad, and wrote what I called A Father's Day Lament, which I posted on social media.

It felt good. Felt like the gap closed a little. And so I want to share it with you, too.

A Father's Day Lament
I know how hard it is for those of us who had crappy fathers, abusive fathers, fathers who weren't there in the way a father is "supposed to be," either because they were absent, flew the coop, or were technically there but always working, or hidden behind a boozy fog or some other, possibly darker, veil.

It can be hard to see everyone celebrating their dads, both living and dead, gushing with good memories, posting the kind of pictures you wish you had of you and your dad.

It's hard because you want to feel happy for those people, you want to like their posts, and you really do feel happy for them—but that happiness is curdled with your own caustic feelings of regret, and so that makes this day even a little sadder for you.

Not being able to fully share in someone else's joy is just another kind of lack.

I've never spoken out about how I feel on Father's Day, but I've felt this way every Father's Day for a long, long time.

And I bet I'm not the only one.

So why post this? Why not do what I usually do and stay off social media today?

Because deep inside there's a little kid, sitting in a pool of sadness, wondering where his dad is.

That hurt little boy is buried beneath layers of anger and cynicism and silence.

And since my own dad is dead, and because he couldn't do it when he was alive, I have to be the one to reach down into that sadness and tilt that little boy's head up to the light and say, "I see you. I'm here for you. I love you."

I get to be for myself the dad I never had.

Maybe that's something worth celebrating.

After I put this post out into the world, a lot of people wrote in to say that this was how they felt on Mother's Day.

And now I'm going to go and let my family take me to brunch.

Happy Father's Day.

226

91

Act Natural

I'm sure at some point you've been in some awkward situation, possibly involved in something inappropriate, or perhaps downright illegal, and someone whispered, with a hushed urgency, "Act natural."

Which is absurd. Because acting is the antithesis of natural.

Don't get me wrong, I think acting is a wonderful gift, and you can make a lot of money, be adored by millions, and win some shiny awards for being great at your craft.

But at some point even the greatest actor wants to drop the act, right?

I mean, who wants to be in a relationship where you're always having to pretend to be someone you're not? Nobody . . . and it doesn't matter if the relationship is with your millions of adoring fans or your wife or parents or boss or . . . anyone.

I think this is also true of what is arguably the most important relationship: the one you have with yourself, with your own mind.

Most people think that meditation involves some kind of manipulation of their mind, trying to have fewer thoughts, or nicer thoughts. Or maybe they like guided meditations, in which they get to replace the voice in their head with someone else's nice, soothing voice.

This makes sense for two reasons:

1. Most people come to meditation because their relationship with their mind has become quite hostile.

2. There are entire spiritual traditions based on manipulating your conscious experience. And they can produce some very real benefits, and some amazing states of consciousness.

But the one state of consciousness you cannot manipulate yourself into is the natural state. You can't focus, or concentrate, or intend, or affirm, or visualize it.

But you can let go of doing and allow meditation to simply be. To unfold with no manipulation, without trying to make anything happen. Just be, with your warty thoughts and all.

It can be challenging, because it flies in the face of everything you've been taught about how to be a good person—that you need to do a good job at everything you do and then figure out how to do it even better next time.

But it's so worth the non-effort.

92

The Source

Man, you don't get happiness from your life,
you bring happiness to your life.
— A really cool old guy I met in my 30s

The other day I was in a long line at the grocery store, looking around, and I guess had a pretty big grin on my face, because as this sour-faced guy cut through the line right in front of me, he gruffly asked, "What're you so happy about?"

He was gone in a flash, so there wasn't really time to reply . . . and I don't think he was really interested in what I might have said. But the answer I would've given was, "No reason."

That wasn't always the case for me. For a big chunk of my life I thought I knew what I needed to make me happy, and I chased it relentlessly. But I was, for far too much of the time, angry and unhappy.

Why?

Because I had a content-based idea of happiness. I thought if I had better stuff, a bigger title, more money, better friends, better food, better travel experiences, etc. that I would be happier.

Sound familiar?

But this idea, that our happiness is somewhere outside of us, contingent upon some condition or some accomplishment, is not only wrong . . . it's dangerous. Because we end up chasing happiness in the world, in the one place where it can never be found. And this fruitless endeavor is actually the source of our unhappiness. This is why there are so many people who have so much—fame, friends, sexual conquests, business success, political power, gadgets, money, etc.—who are utterly miserable. And they make plenty of others miserable in the process.

This is the bad news.

The good news is that we are not empty vessels waiting to be filled by whatever happiness we can squeeze from the husk of this cold, cruel world. The good news is that the opposite is true. That all the happiness and joy and love we've ever experienced in our life has arisen from within. And the better news is that the source is always accessible and renewable. We all, at our core, have a sustainable happiness factory, waiting to be brought online.

Meditation can be a way of reconnecting with the source of that happiness. We sit comfortably, close our eyes, and allow our minds settle. No concentrating or focusing. No acknowledging thoughts and letting them go. And so we fall away from the surface of life, from all the striving and acquiring and accomplishing to the layer of consciousness at which we are already fulfilled. And we emerge rested, energized, and with a greater tendency to be happy for no reason at all—which is the best reason of all.

Learning to meditate doesn't mean that we stop having relationships, or owning stuff, or getting things done. It doesn't mean we don't strive to accomplish things, even big things, or that we don't take pride in those accomplishments. It just means we know that our happiness isn't dependent on those things.

And instead of looking to import happiness, instead of trying so hard to arrange life so that everything lines up perfectly for us be happy, we start to move through life exporting the happiness that flows from within.

It's a nicer, happier way to live.

93

Respect

I was in a "discussion" with our 11-year-old and heard myself saying the same thing parents throughout the ages have said.

"I just want you to respect what I'm saying."

But, to be honest, in that particular moment what I meant was "obey." To stop arguing and do what I said he should do . . . now.

Afterwards I reflected on how often that's really what we mean when we use the word respect.

~~Respect~~ Obey authority.

~~Respect~~ Obey your elders.

~~Respect~~ Obey tradition.

Sounds a little harsh when you put it like that, doesn't it?

The truth is I don't want to raise my kids to be blindly obedient. And so I have to be willing to respect them enough to be open to them disobeying me. To have their own ideas about what to do, how to do it, and when.

I have to remind myself that life is better as a sloppy, often cantankerous, democracy than a nice, tidy dictatorship, maddening though it may sometimes be.

Because obviously my way is the right way . . . right?

Step back from the parent/child dynamic and I think you'll find that often when we feel disrespected we might be showing equal disrespect for the other person's way of doing things.

We believe we're right and they're wrong.

One of the most common complaints of people who cohabitate is that the other person, "Doesn't know how to fold clothes properly."

It's funny . . . but also kind of sad.

Where did we get this crazy idea that if everyone would just do everything the way we want then life would be awesome?

And how can we let it go?

94

At Home

Coming to the end of a month-long trip (Turkey for three weeks and then a week in London), we are all looking forward to coming home.

Last night I was packing, which got to me thinking about home, specifically about what it means to feel at home . . . in the world, in life, in your own skin. And I was reminded of an article I read about 10 years ago, when I was just starting to find my flow as a meditation teacher.

It was about a study in which people were asked to sit in a room, alone, for 6–15 minutes, with only their thoughts. No phone. No fidget spinner. No tattered waiting-room magazines.

The only thing people could do to distract themselves from their thinking was to press a button that would deliver a painful shock to a cuff wrapped around their ankle. How painful? When allowed to test the shock beforehand, people rated it as painful enough that they'd pay money to avoid feeling it again.

Can you guess the results?

After a few minutes alone with their thoughts a significant majority of participants chose to administer the shock. Many people (mostly men) zapped themselves several times. And for those who refrained from pushing the button, most still rated the experience of just sitting there with their thoughts as "extremely unpleasant."

This was a study about how much at home people felt—not when traveling to faraway lands, not even in their own country, but in their own minds. It was a study about how comfortable they were in themselves.

Not very.

There have been thousands of studies showing the benefits of meditation, from lower risk of heart disease, lower blood pressure, relief from PTSD, fewer sick days, better sleep . . . and so on.

I don't remember ever seeing a study about how meditation improves one's ability to simply be at peace with one's thoughts (I think this might be the very definition of inner peace), but I think it might be one of the biggest benefits of them all—to be able to be at ease, without the incessant need to distract, to be at home in oneself anywhere in the world.

Because wherever you go, there you are.

95

The Real Meaning of Success

I used to think success meant winning.

It meant things were going "my way."

And if things weren't going my way, which was often, that meant I was losing. That I was a loser.

Looking at success that way meant I was often frustrated and angry. I would beat myself up, and RESOLVE TO DO BETTER.

You know the drill.

Thankfully, I no longer think of my life in terms of wins and losses. Of failures or successes.

I see that it's all success. And I don't mean that as some sort of starry-eyed, bliss-bunny nonsense.

To understand what I mean we have to expand the word a bit— from success to succession.

As in, "The King is dead! Long live the King!"

Seeing the unfolding of life in this way is the difference between getting stuck, sitting in judgment over what happened, and turning our attention instead to what follows from what happened.

What's great about this approach is that it allows us to flow with life instead of fighting it. And when we stop fighting life we enjoy it more, create more and, ironically, find that we're more "successful."

If you want to see a hilarious example of this principle in action, google Rafael Mantesso Jimmy Choo. Trust me on this one.

96

Unpointed

A student sent me a report from a talk he attended with someone billed as an American Enlightened Master. In response to a question, the Master said that the point of meditation was "to stop the mind."

Yeah, I've heard that before too.

My follow-up question would've been, "And then what?" Because clearly (and thankfully) the mind somehow seems to know how to start itself back up again.

I don't claim to be enlightened (especially not with a capital E), and so you might discount my thoughts on this subject, but . . . what's the deal with trying to reduce everything down to a point? Why does anything, whether it's meditation, or a good meal, or life itself, need to be pinned down so precisely?

Sometimes when people ask me what's the point of meditation, I usually say something like, "To get past the part of you that asks the question." They usually laugh . . . but I'm not joking.

Trying to reduce something down to a single point hasn't worked for science, which despite its quest to pin down the objective truth of everything, has revealed that we can't know anything for certain.

When you go out to dinner at a nice restaurant, is nutrition really the endpoint? Have you ever seen a Yelp review that lists the percentages of RDA nutrients delivered? Is there a point to having kids? Or getting married? Or writing a meditation newsletter?

This radical statement is based on what theoretical physicists call The Uncertainty Principle, which was developed by Werner Heisengberg in 1925. The best book on the topic, especially for non-scientists, is Helgoland by Carlo Rovelli.

The transactional mindset that drives us to be one-pointed, to always be focused on what's in it for me, is the death of good conversation, and of a great many relationships.

We push our mind around all day, telling it what to think, what to focus on. Imagine if you did that with someone you love? How do you think that might affect your relationship? It's no wonder that so many people have such a hostile relationship with their own mind, and think that meditation is the way to tame it.

Life is, thankfully, wonderfully unpointed. It absolutely refuses to be pinned down and, like a wriggly toddler, manages to wrest itself free of all attempts to control it.

Life is a dance, to be enjoyed for its own sake. And in the same way that we don't dance to get to a certain point on the floor, we don't live to come to some single-pointed summation.

I long ago gave up trying to achieve anything in meditation. That doesn't mean that I don't enjoy the benefits of meditating, it just means that when I sit I'm not trying to make anything in particular happen. And meditation is both easier, and more enjoyable, as a result.

The mind, and all its thoughts, is a stream. Stop trying to dam it up.

97

Pain vs. Suffering

It hurts when I wear these shoes. (my wife)
Then don't wear those shoes. (me)
But I like them. (my wife)

> *Pain is essential for the survival of the body, but none compels you to suffer. Suffering is due entirely to clinging or resisting; it is a sign of our unwillingness to move on, to flow with life.*
> — Sri Nisargadatta Maharaj, *I Am That*

Pain, whether physical or emotional, is a signal.

Suffering is what happens when we ignore that signal, when we resist whatever change is necessary to deal with the source of pain.

When we insist on wearing those shoes, or staying in that relationship, or continuing to slog away at a job that's slowly killing us, or (speaking from personal experience here) when we try to make a 13-hour road trip in one day with two young children strapped into car seats.

Why would we do this?

So many reasons. Mostly, I'd suggest it's because we refuse to accept the situation in front of us for what it is. (The trip should really take two days.) And instead of accepting, we try to rationalize the situation or speculate about why we're suffering. We get all tangled up in our thoughts, wondering what it means, why me, thinking what we could've done differently, or whining about what someone else should have done differently.

And deep down, perhaps we suffer because we believe—have in fact been taught by parents/schools/churches to believe—that we deserve to suffer.

Man is born into sin.

Life is suffering.

Suffering is virtue.

A vale of tears.

Blah, blah, blah.

This is not the Vedic worldview. The Veda teaches us that the nature of life is bliss. That suffering is a choice. Our choice not to accept the situation for what it is, but instead to hold on, tenaciously, to how we thought/imagined/hoped things would be. We live in our heads and not in the world, and this is why we suffer.

So how can we choose differently? First, by getting out of our heads. By allowing us to know ourselves as something other than our thoughts and feelings.

One of the great gifts of meditation is that it allows us to know the truth of our essential nature: that beyond our thoughts, our ego, our doubts and our frustrations, we are perfect, whole and complete. We allow our mind to settle to quieter and calmer layers of consciousness, perhaps having an experience of that baseline level of transcendental consciousness at which there are no problems, no speculation, no thinking at all. Just pure, unbounded, blissful silence. And having had that experience, we re-enter the world of thinking and doing with a bit more perspective, a bit more of an ability to accept the situation, any situation, for what it is—temporary.

We are not doomed to suffer. We can change how we feel and act, and in doing so improve both our ability to appreciate the present moment (no matter how painful), and to create for ourselves a better future. And the best part is that it's as easy as finding a comfy chair, closing our eyes, and doing as little as possible. No concentrating, no focusing, just allowing the natural flow of consciousness to take its course. Pure acceptance.

Which is, nicely, the exact opposite of suffering.

98

Don't You Tell Me to Calm Down

Have you ever been really anxious about something . . . perhaps freaking out a bit?

And has someone ever told you, perhaps a tad forcefully, to calm down?

Have you ever told yourself, maybe even yelled at yourself, in your head or actually out loud, to chill the f*#K out?

Did it work? (Insert laughter here.)

Of course it didn't work.

Because it never works.

But have you ever wondered, "Why doesn't it work?"

Because when we're really freaking out, our bodies are flooded with stress chemistry . . . and being yelled at to calm down only makes it worse. So whether it's a well-meaning friend urging us to chill, or our harsh inner critic cracking the whip, we perceive it as a threat, which stimulates another jolt of stress hormones, and the downward spiral pulls us deeper in.

So it can be very hard in the moment to shift our chemistry all the way from anxious to calm.

But what if we don't have to go that far?

In her wonderful book, *First We Make the Beast Beautiful*, Sarah Wilson talks openly and honestly about her life-long experience with anxiety. And she cites a Harvard study in which they asked people experiencing anxiety-charged situations—singing karaoke, giving a speech, taking a math test—to simply say, out loud, "I'm excited! I'm excited! I'm excited!" And then they compared the results to people who were encouraged to take a deep breath and calmly intone the mantra, "I am calm. I am calm. I am calm."

The results? People who consciously sought to reframe their anxiety as excitement performed better. They sang better, spoke better, and got more answers correct than the people who were basically asked to use their minds to override the signals racing through their nervous systems.

I have given Sarah Wilson's book to several of my students who really struggle with anxiety, and have recommended it to many, many more. Check it out if you, or someone you know is dealing with intense anxiety.

Turns out that it's easier to shift from a threat mindset to an opportunity mindset than it is to jump all the way across the chasm from anxious to calm.

Which is good, because who wants to have to make some big, scary leap when you're worried about falling flat on your face?

99

The Power of Yes + And

A friend of mine in Mexico City recently started taking some improv classes, something I had a bit of experience with, decades ago, when I did some workshops with a group called *The Groundlings* in Los Angeles.

In addition to being a lot of fun, improv introduced me to a radical concept called *Yes, and*.

Here's how it works:

Someone enters a scene saying something like, "Aunt Gretchen just turned into a Pegasus!"

And the next person's job is to say something like, "Yes! And lucky I have this saddle handy, because I'm late to work!"

And the next person might say, "Yes! And there's room for the baby seat."

Yes, and is all about affirming what's happening, and then adding to the flow.

It requires the improviser to be open and available to whatever is happening in a scene as it unfolds, no matter how much it might surprise them.

Improv grinds to a painfully awkward halt if, instead of "Yes, and . . ." the next person says, "But . . . no, wait . . . that's not what I thought you were going to say."

So how does this apply in life?

First, we accept that what's happening on the stage of life is indeed what's happening—even though it's not what we might have expected or wanted. We say Yes to life, instead of wallowing in frustration and anger, trapped behind the rigid bars of our expectations.

Then, and this is equally important, we take the energy we would've burned up getting frustrated and angry and use it to adapt.

This doesn't mean we have to be happy about what happened. But it does give us the ability to interact with life, instead of reacting.

More *Yes, and.* Less *But, no.*

It's a fun way to make the audience laugh.

And not a bad way to live.

100

Binge Thinking

Do you ever just allow your head to be filled with your own thoughts?

Or are you usually stuffing it full of other people's ideas? Maybe a podcast, a book, a movie, sports . . . something educational or entertaining, thinking you've got to optimize the time you have available?

Now don't get me wrong, I LOVE a good podcast.

I listen to audiobooks while walking the dog.

I read some kind of book almost every night before bed, and often for a good chunk of time during the day.

And my wife and I enjoy sharing a guilty look as we decide to watch just one more episode of whatever show we're currently crushing on.

But I've discovered how rewarding it can be to spend long stretches of time intentionally NOT filling my head with other people's thoughts.

Sometimes it's when I'm on a walk, or driving with the stereo off, or just gazing out the window, or whatever.

Just me and my thoughts . . . most of them utterly useless and totally unmemorable . . . sometimes for an hour or more.

And that's not just OK, it's kind of the point.

And every now and then some insight arises, some little nub of an original idea, some whispered bit of wisdom from that deep, inner voice that we all have, but often drown out in a flood of streaming content.

If you haven't experimented with flipping the OFF switch on the non-stop stream of content, I highly recommend you give it a try.

Because how can you know what *you* think, if you don't allow yourself *to* think?

Take this simple test: see how long you can go without dipping back into the never-ending stream of streaming content.

101

How to Love What You Hate

(Or at least how to start.)

I was sitting at a café, rereading one of my favorite little books, and listening to the people at the table next to me getting more and more worked up about the latest Trumpian travesty, when I came to this passage:

> One of my psychedelic excursions had gotten off to a bad start, and I was sinking into a really satanic bummer. As I looked about me at people turning evil, shrunken, colorless, old, and weird, I suddenly thought, 'Well, what did you think it was that needed to be loved?' And just like that, the doors opened and I was in paradise.
> — Thaddeus Golas, *The Lazy Man's Guide to Enlightenment*

Boom.

"Well, what did you think it was that needed to be loved?"

That question rocked my world. Maybe not to the euphoric degree as Mr. Golas, but I was sipping coffee and he was high on acid.

I started thinking about Trump, about what it might be like to be him. (Shudder.) I wouldn't want a moment of his internal life. He's in so much pain, how could he not hurt others?

Hating him doesn't help him, or the world, or me.

Darkness cannot drive out darkness; only light can do that.
Hate cannot drive out hate; only love can do that.
— Martin Luther King, Jr.

It's not easy to open our hearts to what disgusts and infuriates us. It's never been easy.

But it is what's needed. It's what's always needed.

I'm strongly opposed to Trump's policies and actions, but I am not anti-Trump the person. I truly feel compassion for him, and hope that he is somehow graced with the opportunity to come to a place of healing before he passes.

251

102

Dancing Animals

People often ask me, "How can I extend the meditative experience into everyday life?"

Usually I get the feeling that they're hoping I'll give them a tip or technique that will allow them to feel some kind of abiding bliss, maybe an expansive, tingly feeling, like they can sometimes experience in deep meditation.

But I think the real answer is much simpler, and a whole lot more practical.

It's to simply allow yourself to be more present, more of the time, for whatever just happens to be flowing over the transom of your experience . . . and to enjoy yourself thoroughly in the process.

Kurt Vonnegut, one of my favorite writers, has a very prosaic way of describing what that might actually be like.

I tell my wife I'm going out to buy an envelope.

"Oh," she says, "well, you're not a poor man. You know, why don't you go online and buy a hundred envelopes and put them in the closet?"

And so I pretend not to hear her. And go out to get an envelope because I'm going to have a hell of a good time in the process of buying one envelope. I meet a lot of people. And see some great looking babies. And a fire engine goes by. And I give them the thumbs up. And I'll ask a woman what kind of dog that is. And, and I don't know. The moral of the story is—we're here on Earth to fart around. And, of course, the computers will do us out of that. And what the computer people don't realize, or they don't care, is we're dancing animals. You know, we love to move around. And it's like we're not supposed to dance at all anymore.

Dancing animals. Here to fart around. Just because.

Not a bad philosophy of life.

And to bring it back to the opening question, I think it's not so much how we can extend meditation into life, it's how meditation can extend our enjoyment of life.

103

In Hiding

I was stopped in traffic yesterday and noticed something that made me snort with laughter. It was a brand-new BMW, a regular old gasoline-powered model, but it had this cleverly designed bumper that obscured the tailpipe from view.

I remember when cars proudly showed off their tailpipes. Because dual, or even quad-exhaust systems with big tailpipes were a kind of virtue signaling that your car was POWERFUL, that the engine was unencumbered by bottled-up exhaust gases, that its stream of pollutants was "free-flowing." When I was 16, I spent a couple hundred dollars, a huge sum at the time, to add a dual-exhaust system to my janky Camaro because I wanted that performance look and sound.

So why would BMW's designers put so much effort into obscuring the tailpipe? Is it because BMW is no longer a performance brand? Of course not. It's because these days more and more people want their performance cars electrified. But if you can't afford one, or don't have a way of charging it? Well then better to tuck the offending exhaust port behind a bit of bumper and hope no one notices.

Now, I get why we care about the image we project into the world. And I'm not saying that we have to flaunt our flaws . . . although I'm sure we all know someone who uses that tactic to get attention.

What I care about is what we try to hide from *ourselves*, the inner ickiness we feel ashamed of, and how the energy we put into hiding distorts who and how we are in the world.

That psychic strain is certainly why so many social media influencers are clinically depressed. But even we less-photogenic folks suffer when we try so hard to obscure what we don't want others to see.

Because you can't hide the truth about yourself from yourself.

You might try denial, or booze, or sex. You might try tuning your chakras so that all your vibrations are high, or visualizing your happy place, or sticking post-it notes with uplifting affirmations all over your house. But deep, deep down . . . you know.

In German they have a great word, that I can spell, but probably not pronounce, *hintergedanken*, which means a thought that nags at you from way, way, way back in the back of your mind, but you can't get rid of.

One of the most powerful (but admittedly scary) things about true meditation is that if you simply sit and allow any and all thoughts to arise . . . they will. Especially *those* thoughts.

But when we learn to allow we take the first step towards acknowledging.

We stop hiding from ourselves.

It might not be pretty. But where it leads is beautiful.

My favorite essay about how the futility of trying to fool ourselves is On Self Respect, by Joan Didion. Definitely worth a read.

104

Thanksreceiving

It is good to give thanks, to be grateful, and not just on the fourth Thursday in November.

But as much as we benefit from being more grateful, I think it's worth considering how much brighter the world might be made if we all upped our receiving game the rest of the year.

Meaning when someone gives us a compliment, or offers to pick up the check, or maybe to go out their way to do us a favor, that we graciously accept . . . as opposed to what we too often do which is to demur, deflect, or flat out refuse.

No, I can't let you do that . . . let's split it.
That's too much trouble.
Well, that's nice of you to say but . . .
Oh, I wouldn't want to bother you.
You shouldn't have . . . it's too much.

And so on.

Something very beautiful, and tangible, is squandered when a gift is declined.

There is a dimming of energy you can both feel.

You give someone a great gift when you graciously allow yourself to accept theirs.

105

The Folly of
Single-Pointed Focus

A lot of people come to learn meditation because they think it will help them improve their focus. Because they believe that being able to be stay intensely focused on one thing will help unlock their best selves, make them better at their jobs, and help them live a better life.

But I don't think it works that way. I think focus is overrated.

Try this exercise: pick any object and focus on it intently for 60 seconds. Really concentrate, keep your eyes locked, and try to notice every little detail. OK . . . go.

Tiring, isn't it?

I bet that after only 30 seconds or so you probably started to feel tension around the eyes and in your jaw. Keep at it much longer and you might get a slight headache.

Next, take the same object and just allow your gaze to fall upon it. Don't focus or concentrate at all. Allow the muscles around your eyes to be relaxed.

OK . . . go.

Much easier, isn't it?

And notice that you are able to see just as much about the object, that you pick up just as many if not more details, when you simply allow yourself to see it as opposed to focusing and concentrating.

Control and effort are the opposites of flow.

When an athlete is in the zone, when they have "eyes in the back of their head," it's not because they are intently focused on one thing, but because they are wide open to everything.

I think this is what we really want. To be fully immersed in the fullness of the moment, without trying to be. Not to be in control of life, but to be consciously in flow with it as it unfolds.

You can approach meditation as a way of disciplining the mind. Focusing, concentrating, trying to hold the perfect posture, steeling your will to wall yourself off from distractions . . .

Or you can approach it as a way of freeing the mind, as a way of opening to everything as it unfolds—thoughts, noises, sensations—resisting nothing.

This is the difference between meditation practices that cultivate what I call wide-angle, present-moment awareness instead of single-pointed focus. Being more widely aware actually leads to better performance, and more enjoyable experiences. That's what makes being in a flow state so desirable, being fully absorbed in life, instead of intensely focused on a small part of life, like a laser pointer.

Now don't get me wrong, if you have to navigate a complicated PowerPoint presentation, a laser pointer can be useful.

But I wouldn't want to be one.

The Benefit(s) of the Doubt

There are two.

The first is when someone gives us the benefit of the doubt.

We get the chance to be heard, to be seen, to be trusted . . . if only for a while longer than we might have expected.

It's nice when that happens.

But it's worth considering what we get from extending the benefit of the doubt to others.

We get to shuck off the brittle armor of our certainty.

We get the chance to be proven wrong about something, or someone.

And if that should happen?

Then we get the benefit of growth.

And the circle of our trust gets a little wider.

So . . .

With whom, or in what situation, might you be able to reap the benefits of doubt?

107

Laundry Day

The first place I taught meditation was above a laundromat. So my students and I got to enjoy the lulling hum of commercial washers and dryers as we meditated.

We also got to see a lot of people struggling under the weight of giant bags of laundry. If you don't have a washing machine at home, you know what I'm talking about. If you do, maybe you can remember the sling-it-over-the-shoulder "ugh" of laundry day.

When we have to go somewhere to do our laundry, even if it's just down to the shared machines in the basement of our apartment complex, it tends to pile up.

And pile up.

And then finally we have to do something about it.

It was surely in an effort to put off the hassle of doing laundry for just one more day that some guy invented the "sniff test."

When we learn to meditate it's like getting a washing machine. Because we have this wonderful new tool we can use to easily launder ourselves of the day's stresses. The little (and sometimes not so little) things that frustrate, frazzle and just plain wear us out.

The irrational client or boss, the super-slow cashier, the dog poop on the sidewalk, the kids that refuse to put on their shoes, the driver who cuts us off, insomnia, the _____ (insert your own daily source of aggravation).

But when we don't have a convenient way to do that, things tend to pile up. And the load of that accumulating stress wears us down.

It's why we call Wednesday "hump day," because after only a few days of work we're already struggling.

It's why the expression TGIF (Thank God It's Friday) even exists.

It's why people who go on vacation spend the first couple of days "decompressing."

Imagine how much you might enjoy your vacations if you didn't get so "compressed" in the first place.

Imagine how much you might enjoy the rest of your life, even when not on vacation.

Imagine you, without your stress, when every day can be a kind of laundry day.

108

The Stronger the Light, the Sharper the Shadow

When I was a kid, a common insult might be to say of some skittish boy, "He's afraid of his own shadow."

But aren't we all?

Aren't we all just a bit afraid of whatever might be buried beneath all those positive affirmations, by what's pushed just out of frame in our oh-so-carefully-curated social media feeds?

Isn't this a big part of why so many fabulously famous actors and entertainers struggle with depression and addiction?

A meditation teacher I used to follow once punched his wife in the face in an argument that started when she didn't want to have sex. Or at least that's what the police report says.

Can you imagine what it costs him psychologically to keep that hidden behind the ever-lengthening beard, the beads and the saffron robes he's taken to wearing more and more?

One of the most illuminating things about the expansion of awareness is that it makes it harder and harder to ignore what we don't want to admit about ourselves.

The stronger the light, the sharper the shadow.

Because I post these little essays every Monday, many assume that I'm writing from a place where I've got it all figured out. This is laughably far from true.

As the old Zen saying goes, "If you want to know the level of attainment of the master . . . ask the wife."

I'm certainly a few steps further along the path than when I started, but I often find myself writing about things that I'm dealing with myself.

I write them for me as much as I do for you.

The difference, and it's a big one, is that I'm better able to observe myself and my failings, often at a level of granular detail, without whipping out the excoriating lash of self-loathing.

I used to be very hard on myself, and not in a good way.

Perhaps you know someone this can be said of.

Perhaps that someone is you.

If so, you might find this quote from J. Krishnamurti helpful:

> *The ability to observe without judgment is the highest form of intelligence.*

I still get caught up in self-judgment now and then . . . but I manage to free myself a lot more quickly.

What about you?

109

Play Your Cards

I am totally confident, not that the world will get better, but that we should not give up the game before all the cards have been played. The metaphor is deliberate; life is a gamble. Not to play is to foreclose any chance of winning. To play, to act, is to create at least a possibility of changing the world.
— Howard Zinn, Historian

Whenever the current chaos passes.

Whatever the next normal ends up being.

When people sift through their memories of these tumultuous times.

What small act of yours will they remember?

Will it be because you called?

Because you helped?

Because you showed unexpected kindness/patience/care?

Because you didn't give in to pessimism?

Because you _____?

I can't fill in the blank.

But you can.

I wrote this one during the pandemic (remember that?), but I find it's just as relevant now. Hope you agree.

110

You First

Outside the market the other day a guy and I engaged in a brief round of trying to out-polite each other.

"You first," we both said, gesturing magnanimously toward the door. There was a bit of herky-jerky awkwardness as we each waited for the other to go, then we both started to step forward at the same time, and then stopped after seeing the other had started, until we both laughed and realized the doorway was wide enough to allow us both to pass side-by-side . . . so we did.

And it made me think.

There are many situations, like the one above, where it really doesn't matter who goes first. But what about the situations in which who goes first seems to be of critical importance?

Like when we get into a heated exchange with someone we care about, with truly regrettable things being said on both sides, we dig in our heels and indignantly insist that they be the first to say, "I'm sorry."

Or in new romantic relationships, we can hold ourselves back, not wanting to risk being hurt, waiting for the other person to be the first to say, "I love you."

Or, when someone has done us wrong we stubbornly insist that they own up to their error, perhaps even grovel before us, before we grant them the blessing of our forgiveness.

The forgiveness thing used to be so hard for me. Then I read something, I forget where.

> *Forgiveness is letting go of all hope for a better past.*
> — Anonymous

I thought, "Damn, that's good."

And the embittered shell I'd encased myself in cracked, just a little.

It became easier for me to stop insisting that other people take responsibility, and start taking it for myself.

Is there someone you're waiting on, to do or say something, so that you can move on?

What if you stopped waiting?

What if you went first?

111

The Joy of Missing Out

I went to a wedding this weekend. In the mountains, outside, under the trees. It was a beautiful, joyful occasion.

Two wonderful people, wonderfully in love, surrounded by family and friends, declaring their decision to settle for this one person, completely giving up the hope of finding someone better.

Wait . . . what? Settle?

Yes. Because what is the commitment of marriage if not the joyful declaration that you are forgoing the prospect of something better? You are choosing this person, to have and to hold, in sickness and in health . . . and in doing so, you're okay with taking a pass on everyone else.

In a world plagued by FOMO (the fear of missing out for those not familiar with the acronym), marriage, like all big decisions, is a declaration of JOMO, the joy that can only come from being willing to miss out on everyone, and everything else the world might offer you.

A couple years ago I wrote a related post about JOBP, the Joy of Being Present, as the opposite of FOMO.

But watching my two friends get hitched this weekend, I realized that it's impossible to be present if you're always hedging your bets, keeping your options open.

The truth is that when you decide to do anything, you automatically cut yourself off from a whole world of things you could've done instead.

The root of "decide" is from the Latin -*cidere*, which means to cut. Every decision you make is a surgical act.

But life isn't just about making choices. It's about having the courage to fully commit to those choices.

And what do you get in return? The joy that can only come from making such a commitment.

And this applies to what you're going to do in the next hour, or who you're going to partner with on the long road of life.

You can't do everything, or date everyone.

And why on Earth would you want to try?

112

Can You Hear the Music?

I've been cutting way back on social media for the last several months . . . posting less and reading less . . . but the other night I dipped in and got lost down a rabbit hole of doom. War brewing with Iran, all of Australia on fire, the homelessness epidemic, corruption, racism, terrorism, corporatism—anywhere and anytime you choose to look you can find ample evidence that the world is going to hell.

And it's at these times I'm reminded of a little book written by the great American composer Aaron Copland, *What to Listen For in Music*.

In it Copland lays out his idea of musical sophistication. He says that for very unsophisticated listeners the scales themselves are music—one note, followed by another note, and then another, progressing up and down at regular intervals, with no surprises whatsoever.

But as our level of sophistication begins to evolve the scales become b-o-r-i-n-g. We can appreciate a bit more surprise, a bit more dissonance. This is the level at which the songs that preschoolers love live. Rise a bit more in sophistication, and you get into the territory of good pop songs. Keep going and we can enjoy the way a jazz soloist can take a melody and stretch and pull it so that it's just barely there. Take the next step and you can appreciate how a classical composer can weave a thematic element through all the movements of a symphony. And so on . . .

Essentially, what Copeland says is that our degree of musical sophistication is simply a measure of how much discordance we can experience without completely losing the thread of the underlying melody.

This is also what the Veda teaches us about life. That the universe is one, whole conscious thing and that we are all expressions of that consciousness. And the thing that this one consciousness is always doing is evolving. This is what Darwin tells us about biology. It's what astrophysicists tell us about the universe. The river is always flowing towards the sea. Sometimes it has to bend itself around a boulder, sometimes a dam may block its path for a while, but it's always flowing. Everything evolves. Everything progresses.

So the question is how good can we be at hearing the evolution of that underlying melody? How can we refine our ability to detect the faint stirrings of progressive change even when things seem to be going to hell all around us, whether in our own lives or the world?

Meditation helps a lot. Journaling can also be good. Talking with a trusted friend (very different than finding someone to complain to) also works.

Personally, I like to reflect back on some of the times in my life when something truly terrible happened . . . and how those ended up being one of those "the worst thing that ever happened was the best thing" stories—like how my wife and I endured a heart-breaking miscarriage at 5 months that led to us turn to adoption, which led to us being the proud parents of two wonderful boys.

So I don't know what will work for you. But I suggest anything that helps you step back from the intensity of the moment and get some perspective.

Anything that helps you hear the music.

113

On Boundaries, Borders and Walls

This question came up in our meditation community a couple weeks ago:

"Hey James, when we have individuals in our lives who do not meditate or handle or cope with stressful situations and try to drag or pull us into their stressful situation . . . how does one handle it?"

What a *great* question. And a very topical one, given that it was the holiday season and people were heading off, either across town or across the country, to be packed around the table with the people who could push their buttons and drag them into drama in ways that only family can.

The discussion that followed focused on the necessity of setting good boundaries, of protecting one's peace, of finding compassion for others, being more patient and less reactive—all things lots of people struggle with. And even though the question was initially addressed to me, I pretty much sat back and watched as a beautiful, wise and loving conversation unfolded. Here are a few snippets to give you a sense of it:

"Boundaries are the distance at which I can love you and me simultaneously."

So good, right?

"The only people who get upset when you start setting boundaries are the ones who benefited from you not having them."

Can I get an Amen?

"To detach isn't to stop caring about others; it means I care equally as much for myself. It means I love myself enough to stay out of others' insanity."

Like I said, I loved watching the conversation unfold, without feeling like I needed to add anything.

But by the time our next Sunday Sangha meditation rolled around, I'd had some time to think more deeply about why we struggle with setting boundaries, and was reminded of a Robert Frost poem, *Mending Wall*, which begins with the line:

Something there is that doesn't love a wall.

And I think that gets to the heart of it.

Because even though we may really need boundaries, we don't love them. It sucks to have to wall off our lives into well-defended partitions, especially from those we're close to. It feels good to be able to feel safe enough to let our guard down.

Which is why we have to be careful that the walls we build between ourselves and others don't get too high, too impenetrable, or too permanent.

The whole poem is worth a read, especially to see how his neighbor just doesn't get what Frost is talking about.

So if you're sitting around the table and someone you've managed to set a solid boundary with says something that triggers you in a negative, hurtful way? Well, then you might have to get up and leave the table and go for a walk.

But what if the wall is so heavily reinforced that you can't really see the other person or notice how they might have changed?

What if the thing they say triggers a giggle? Or brings back a warm memory from some shared experience long before the relationship degraded to the point where boundary-setting was required?

In those situations I think the real skill is in admitting that it might be time to start taking down the wall, because you realize that it's no longer necessary, either because the other person has changed, or because you have.

114

That Floaty Thing

No one ever says to a lifeguard:

Don't throw me the floaty thing . . . can't you see I'm too busy drowning?

But people say stuff like this to meditation teachers all the time:

I'm too stressed to meditate.
I have no time.
There's too much going on.
Maybe when things calm down.

I get it.

In fact, I said it.

Right before I learned to meditate I almost didn't. Because my life was a hot mess. I had a terrible, high-stress job I was on the verge of losing. I had an amazing wife I was on the verge of losing. I was failing as a dad and as a husband. I was drinking too much and wasting too much time on stupid video games.

I was convinced I couldn't meditate, no way, no how, and certainly not *now*.

And then I discovered that I could, even with all that crap going on in my life and my head.

Meditation became my lifesaver.

And now, in the most delightfully astonishing turn of events, I get to throw the floaty thing to you.

115

Finders Keepers

The Universe buries strange jewels deep within us all, and then
stands back to see if we can find them.
— Elizabeth Gilbert

Who doesn't love a good treasure hunt?

Easter eggs are enormously fun to find, whether you're a little kid racing around the yard, or a gamer amped up on some uber-caffeinated energy drink.

There's just something about being on the hunt that makes us more alive. Looking for clues, the excitement of the search, the agony of dead ends, and finally, the joy of discovery.

Well, what if we approached life like that, but with the idea, as Gilbert suggests, that the treasure is hidden within us?

We'd have to be open to discovery, even (or especially) if we've gotten on in years and think we know everything.

We'd have to be willing to follow clues to see where they led, often well off the beaten path of our expectations. And we'd have to be able to bounce back when we hit a dead end. We'd have to never give up until the treasure was found.

A couple days a week my wife, Yvette, teaches art in an assisted-living home. One woman, in her mid-80s, had never painted before. And she LOVES it. "I had no idea I could paint!" she told Yvette, filled with joy at the discovery. "You made my day!"

Which, of course, made Yvette's day.

Happy hunting

116

Goal-Oriented

The goal of incarnate life is to be in love with the world.
— Carl Jung

Sometimes it's easy to be in love. Spectacular sunsets. Biting into a perfectly ripe peach. Puppies playing on the beach.

Sometimes it's harder.

Much, much harder.

But as long as we're alive, being in love with the world is still a damn fine goal.

And the only obstacle, the "goalie" if you will, is our frustration and despair that things he way we believe they have to be for us to be in love with life.

But things are as they are, and the only world in which love can be found is the one that exists, not the one in our heads.

The only time we can be happy is now, and I mean right now, not later.

I know there will be times when pithy reminders like this will fall flat, will be no more than spiritual platitudes, when middle fingers will be flipped up in anger. This week might be one of those times for you, especially if you're on the sensitive side.

It's a great gift to be a sensitive person, to feel the world fully.

The risk, especially in tumultuous times, is being overwhelmed.

So we might be tempted to do things to numb ourselves, or we might try to turn away, to block what's happening.

Now, I'm not saying you can't have a drink now and then, or that you shouldn't go for a nice walk in a beautiful place, or just sit on your porch listening to birds . . . anything to tear yourself from doom-scrolling through the torrent of 24/7 Breaking News!

But be careful.

Because we cannot selectively numb. When we try to turn down the sensitivity dial to protect ourselves from what threatens to overwhelm us we also numb ourselves to what can uplift and enrich us.

And when we put up a dam to block what's happening, the pressure builds and builds until . . .

All dams break.

So what can we do?

While walking our dog on the beach this morning I was reminded of a lovely, quirky film called *JoJo Rabbit* (set in Nazi Germany, of all places/times), about a very sensitive little boy's experiences — some hilarious, others horrific.

The film ends with two lines from the poem *Go to the Limits of Your Longing* by Rainer Maria Rilke:

Let everything happen to you: beauty and terror.
Just keep going. No feeling is final.

The whole poem is worth your time, and the movie too, if you haven't seen it.

117

The Pursuit of Wholeness

The pursuit of happiness seems to me a really dangerous idea and has led to a contemporary disease in Western society, which is fear of sadness . . . I'd like just for a year to have a moratorium on the word "happiness" and to replace it with the word "wholeness." Ask yourself, 'is this contributing to my wholeness?'
— Hugh Mackay, *The Good Life*

This week I'm teaching a woman who, the day before our first session, had to make the awful, heart-wrenching decision to put her dog down. And so she sits in meditation, awash with grief, wondering when she'll get to the bliss that everyone talks about.

"When you allow the grief to wash through you," is the only answer I can give.

Dogs fill up such a big space in our hearts that the hole left behind when they pass is huge. But, and I say this as someone who only a few months ago had to sit on the cold linoleum floor of the vet's office, with tears flowing down my face, holding our wonderful dog Falcon as an injection brought his happy, too-short life to an end, you *really* wouldn't want it to be any other way.

There is no grief without love, and so to love a dog, to love anything, to love life itself is to guarantee there will be times of profound sadness.

Sadness is part of the good life.

Awkwardness too.

The other day our 12-year-old asked my wife, "Mom . . . is it normal to be nervous when you're talking to someone you like?"

How sweet is that? Of course it's normal. And so is his inevitable heartbreak. There's a part of me that wants to protect him from that. But would you really want your kid to go through life never having their heart broken?

We have a natural instinct to want things to be easy. For us and the ones we love. We seek comfort. We want to lessen pain.

But a painless life is not a whole one.

The dullest story ever would be one in which things were great. Then got better. And then got even better. The end.

I didn't sign up for dull. Did you?

A Parting Thought . . .

Our revels now are ended. These our actors,
As I foretold you, were all spirits, and
Are melted into air, into thin air:
And like the baseless fabric of this vision,
The cloud-capp'd tow'rs, the gorgeous palaces,
The solemn temples, the great globe itself,
Yea, all which it inherit, shall dissolve,
And, like this insubstantial pageant faded,
Leave not a rack behind. We are such stuff
As dreams are made on; and our little life
Is rounded with a sleep.
— Prospero, William Shakespeare, *The Tempest*

Acknowledgements

There are so many people I want to thank for their contributions to this book:

First, to Chad Rea, for your blog post about Vedic Meditation which intrigued me enough to think that maybe, just maybe I should try meditation again.

To Jonni Pollard, for urging me to stick with teacher training when I was feeling like an imposter.

To Light Watkins for your friendship, encouragement, and for setting an example of what's possible when you self-publish your first book.

To Jeff Kober, for your wise counsel as I navigated some pretty choppy waters, and to being an example of teaching with integrity

To all the readers of my weekly *monday meditations* posts for encouraging me, repeatedly over the years, to collect them into a book.

To Margaret Lukens and Tim Brunelle for your invaluable editorial feedback that helped me sift through several hundreds of essays to decide which to include in this collection . . . and double thanks to Margaret for proofreading.

To Christine Kawaii for coming up with the title, and for all your support and encouragement.

To my designer Molly Mortimer, and the team at Mayfly Design in Minneapolis, for making it all look great.

To my wife, Yvette, for believing in me, and for being OK with me coming to bed really, really late most Sunday nights while I sat up writing posts that would be sent out the next morning. And thanks also for being OK with me talking about our personal lives in this very public way.

And lastly, I want to express my gratitude for two men who are probably more responsible than anyone for my learning to meditate, and for becoming a teacher.

To Christian, if I hadn't met you I probably wouldn't have learned to meditate. You seemed so *normal*, not at all what I thought a meditation teacher would be . . . and you were even, like me, a baseball fan.

And thanks to Thom for starting the Vedic Meditation community, for approving my application for teacher training, and for years of encouragement and advice as I navigated the first few years as a teacher.

I love you both and am so grateful for the roles you played in my life, even as my teaching has flowed in very different direction.

Bibliograph-ish

This is not a scholarly work, and so a proper bibliography seemed not right. But I do want give credit where credit is due, and also to add some detail about how some of the essays came together:

#1 — *When an Egg Cracks From the Inside* was inspired by a hilarious experience I had attending a Tony Robbins event.

#2 — *Your Flavor of Yummy* is based on teaching a day-long meditation workshop at The Battery SF with my friend Susan O'Connell.

#7 — *No Mistakes* is based on an interview with Herbie Hancock I stumbled across on YouTube that made me appreciate Miles Davis's artistry even more . . . as if that was possible.

#10 — *You Can't Be Serious* includes a quote from G.K. Chesterton that Alan Watts referenced in one of his amazing talks.

#15 — *On Becoming Unoffendable* starts with a quote from a character played by Robert De Niro in Martin Scorsese's incredible film, *Taxi Driver.*

#20 — *Gift Wrapping* includes a line from Shakespeare's *Hamlet,* who might well be literature's first emo character.

#24 — *An Unfair Comparison* took place at the Zen Center of Los Angeles, which is a wonderful teaching institution that has helped many, many people find their way along the spiritual path. I want to make sure to acknowledge that I simply wasn't ready for the instruction they were offering.

#26 — *Falling Awake* echoes the teaching of my favorite teacher, Adyashanti, who used this exact same metaphor comparing awakening with sleeping. I started listening to his talks, and reading his books when I became so disillusioned with my teacher that I wondered if I should even continue teaching. When I discovered Adya's clear, distinct voice I was pleasantly surprised to see that many of the ways he talked about things were insights I had come to on my own . . . and what that taught me is that maybe I did have something to offer. There are many essays in this collection that were inspired, either directly, or tangentially, by his teaching.

#32 — *On the Inherent Interest of Twisty Paths* references an amazing TED Talk by Brené Brown on the topic of vulnerability. If you got anything out of that essay I urge you to go watch her talk.

#33 — *No One Completes You* owes much to my colleague Jeff Kober's writings and talking about relationships. If you are interested in taking a deep dive into the well of Vedic wisdom you should visit jeff-kober.com and sign up for his *Vedic Meditation Thought for the Day* newsletter and/or read his excellent book, *Embracing Bliss*.

#37 — *Afraid of the Dark* contains a reference to *Spiritual Bypassing,* a term that was coined by John Welwood, a Buddhist teacher and psychotherapist, in the early 1980s. It's critical concept to keep in mind as we make our way along the spiritual path, and reinforces the importance of shadow work.

#40 — *Do Gooder* includes a line from the Bhagavad Gita, a book I can't recommend highly enough for anyone interested in the intersection of spirituality and daily life. There are many great translations, but I would avoid the one by Maharishi Mahesh Yogi that's put out by the TM organization . . . unless you want to laugh at how someone could so ham-fistedly inject the trademarked phrase Transcendental Meditation™ again and again and again into one of the world's great spiritual texts.

#42 — *It's No Thing* is inspired by Alan Watts, the most wonderfully articulate and playful voice in spirituality. (Although Anthony de Mello is also up there.) The essay includes a line from a great song by The Beatles, who learned to mediate and helped, through their advocacy, millions of others to do the same. Namaste.

#45 — *Behind the Mask* is also inspired by Alan Watts.

#46 — *Loosen Your Grip* includes a quote from the incomparable Rumi, which makes this as good a time as any to recommend any of the many translations of the Sufi mystic poet's work by Coleman Barks . . . who's a great poet in his own right.

#50 — *Filling the Hole* is inspired by my experiences attending AA meetings with my dad, which is where I got to see a side of him—helpful, wise, funny—that I never got to see growing up. My dad is the one who gave me Craig Nakken's book, which I recommend for anyone who thinks, "Hey . . . I'm not an addict." Because most of us are addicted to something.

#52 — *Enthusiasm* contains a passing reference to Joseph Campbell. If you haven't read *The Hero with a Thousand Faces*, or seen the series of interviews Campbell did with Bill Moyers, *Joseph Campbell and the Power of Myth*, you should really check them out.

#55 — *Like a Tree, Not a Pillow* introduced me to the deeply soulful poetry of Jane Hirshfield, who, like Mary Oliver, writes with such reverence for the natural world.

#59 — *Dis-Ease*, and all the related essays that deal with my wife's medical journey are as good a time as any to express my deep appreciation for the loving care and skill of the entire lung transplant team at UCSF and the Pulmonology Department at Kaiser.

#62 — *Heavenly* includes a quote from the wonderful Matsui Basho, and another from The Gospel of Thomas, one of the Gnostic Gospels, which are not included in the traditional bible . . . but really should be. If anyone is interested in looking at the teachings of Jesus through the lens of non-duality I recommend *Resurrecting Jesus,* by Adyashanti.

#65 — *Spoiler Alert* is a tip of the cap to Alan Watts, one of my absolute favorites. He's a great writer, but a better speaker, and so if you have a chance to listen to his books you won't be disappointed. I recommend the audio book *You're It!* as a great place to get started.

#66 — *Plowing the Field* is my take on a traditional Vedic metaphor to describe meditation. I'm glad I had it handy to explain what I do to my cousins.

#67 — *The Opposite of Gonzo* uses another classic metaphor that I love, and use frequently, but can't take credit for.

#75 — *Breath Taking* ends with a quote from the last great acknowledged master of the Vedic tradition, who's more commonly referred to by his nickname (don't you love that spiritual masters can have nicknames?), Guru Deva. I used to not think that much of this quote, even though it's often tossed about in Vedic circles, until my wife's lung transplant made it particularly poignant.

#85 — *Does it Really Matter* opens with a bit of dialog from the delightful *Alice's Adventures in Wonderland,* which is a delightfully surreal story that's worth reading as an adult.

#87 — *You Are Here* is based on what most people would think of a non-quote from one of America's most iconoclastic writers. I know that a lot of people think that to learn about deep spiritual wisdom you have to go to the East, but I think Thoreau, along with Walt Witman, Aldous Huxley and Herman Melville show that there's a lot of wisdom to be found in the West, too.

#88 — *A Beautiful Distortion* ends with a long quote from Mary Ruefle, whose *Madness, Rack & Honey* is one of my top five favorite books.

#89 — *As If* opens with a quote from Adyashanti, the teacher who has had the most impact on my understanding, and who also serves as a role model for teaching with integrity without dogma, and without being tied to tradition.

#97 — *Pain vs. Suffering* includes a quote from Sri Nisargadatta Maharaj's non-dual classic, *I Am That.* The book is a collection of transcribed talks the master gave in his small, cramped apartment, answering the questions of whomever showed up. Highly recommended.

#98 — *Don't You Tell Me to Calm Down* includes a reference to a study I read about in Sarah Wilson's wonderful book, *First We Make the Beast Beautiful,* which is the best book about anxiety I've ever read.

#101— *How to Love What You Hate* starts with a long quote from one of my favorite books, The Lazy Man's Guide to Enlightenment, but Thaddeus Golas. It's not just a great book, but the story of how it came to be written, and published, is wonderful.

#102 — *Dancing Animals* includes a story from one of my favorite writers, Kurt Vonnegut. If you haven't read any of his works I suggest starting with *Slaughterhouse-Five*, a book that is far funnier, and more touchingly human than the title would suggest.

#108 — *The Stronger the Light, the Sharper the Shadow* ends with a terse quote from J. Krishnamurti, one of the most insightful, but uncompromising, teachers I've come across. Not for everyone, but worth checking out.

#109 — *Play Your Cards* opens with a quote from the legendary historian Howard Zinn. To be honest, I'm not a fan of his take on American history, but was delighted to see that this quote was from him.

#112 — *Can You Hear the Music?* is a great example of how some of the most deeply spiritual insights come from books you wouldn't find in spiritual bookstores. Thanks Mr. Copland!

#113 — *Boundaries, Borders and Walls* is about an insight that was inspired by one of Robert Frost's poems. I know you were probably forced to read Frost in school, but he's a much deeper, darker poet than your middle or high-school teacher might have led you to believe. Definitely worth taking another look.

#115 — *Finders Keepers* is based on a wonderful gem of a quote from Elizabeth Gilbert. I never read *Eat, Pray, Love* but absolutely love her TED Talk *Your Elusive Creative Genius*.

#116 — *Goal-Oriented* includes snippets from two people who have, in their own ways, plumbed the depths of what it means to be human: psychologist Carl Jung and poet Rainer Maria Rilke.

#117 — *The Pursuit of Wholeness* opens with a great quote from Australian psychologist Hugh McKay. I think this notion of wholeness vs. happiness is worth reflecting on deeply and so I thought it was a good essay to close the collection.

I have no idea if anyone will actually read through this long list of notes, but if you did, I want to end by saying thank you . . . yes, you.

Hi, I'm James Brown

No, not *that* James Brown. I'm also not the most overtly spiritual guy you'll ever meet, and my wife and kids refuse to let me take myself too seriously. I probably joke around and swear more than your typical meditation/spiritual teacher.

I teach from my own real-world experience, without dogma, with humor when possible, and without tossing around a lot of Sanskrit or ancient Buddhist terminology.

For years I've written a weekly essay about the intersection of meditation and life, because if meditation doesn't work in the context of your busy, noisy life then what's the point?

This is my first book. If you like it, let me know.

With love, James

To learn more about what and how I teach visit vedicpathmeditation.com

www.ingramcontent.com/pod-product-compliance
Lightning Source LLC
Chambersburg PA
CBHW030909120626
46554CB00001B/71